After Suicide Loss:
Coping With Your Grief
2nd Edition

Jack Jordan, Ph.D.
Bob Baugher, Ph.D.

Caring People Press
Newcastle, Washington

After Suicide Loss:
Coping With Your Grief
2nd Edition

Copyright © 2016 by Jack Jordan and Bob Baugher

Table of Contents

Impact

The First Days, Weeks, and Months After a Suicide 1

Your Reactions 3
Your Body – Shock 3
Your Mind – Confusion, Denial, and WHY? 4
Your Emotions – The Roller Coaster 6

Some Specific Challenges 10
Witnessing the Suicide or Finding the Body 10
The Police Investigation 11
The Hospital 12
The People Around You 12
Viewing the Body of Your Loved One 12
Deciding What to Tell Other People 15
The Reactions of Other People 15
Dealing with the Media 17
The Suicide Note 18
(Re)Visiting the Scene of the Suicide 19
The Funeral or Memorial Service 20

If It Was a Friend Who Died of Suicide 21

Self-Care at the Beginning 23
Self-Care of Your Body 24
Self-Care of Your Mind 26
Self-care of Your Spirit 28
Review of Grief Reactions 30

Absorbing the Blow

The First Year and Beyond 31

What to Expect as Your Grief Evolves 31
Expect Waves or Cycles 31
Expect it to take longer than you want 33

Changes in Your Relationships with Others 34
Your Marriage or Partnership 34
Special Problems in a Marriage after a SuicideLoss 36

Your Children 40
  Young Children 40
  Having the Actual Conversation with your Young Child 42
  Guilt & Magical Thinking in Children 45
  Other Emotions and Behavior Your Child May Show 46
  Elementary School Age Children (6 – 12) 47
  The Emergence of the "Why?" Question 49
  Religious Views of the Afterlife and Suicide 49
  School 50
  Adolescents (Ages 13 – 18) 52
  Loss of a Parent, Sibling, or other Relative to Suicide 53
  Loss of a Friend or Peer to Suicide 56
  Longer Term Effects of Childhood Exposure to a Suicide 58
  Take Care of Yourself to Take Care of Your Child 60
  Your Friends and Work Colleagues 61
  Lost Friendships 64

Other Issues in the First Year and Beyond 64
  Finding Longer Term Support: Support Groups & Resources 67
  What Can I Expect from a Bereavement Support Group? 68
  Other Types of Survivor-to-Survivor Contact 69

Surviving

Learning to Live with Your Loss Over Time 71

Into the Second Year and Beyond 71
  Depression & Grief 72
  Suicidality in Survivors: Are You at Risk for Suicide Now? 74
  Your World View is Changing 75
  "Don't Waste Your Grief!" – Post Traumatic Growth 76

Coping Over the Longer Term 78
  Continuing Bonds After Suicide 80
  Feeling (or Not Feeling) the Presence of Your Loved One 81
  Suicide and Your Spirituality 82
  Atheism or Agnosticism 84
  Learning to Carry the Loss Going Forward 84

Conclusion 89

Survivor Narratives

Stories of Hope and Healing 90

Appendices

Appendix A: Seeking Professional Help 121
Deciding to Seek Therapy 121
What Should I Look for in a Therapist? 122
What Grief Counseling Can and Cannot Do 125
Medication 130

Appendix B: Understanding Suicide: The Perfect Storm 133
Suicide Epidemiology in the USA 133
What Causes Suicide? 134
Can Suicide Be Prevented? 136

Appendix C: Military, Fire, or EMT Suicide 139

Appendix D: Supporting a Survivor of Suicide Loss 141

Appendix E: Someone Being Suicidal (Including Yourself) 143
Risk of Suicide in Survivors 144
Risk Factors for Suicide 145
Warning Signs of Imminent Risk 146
Steps to Take If You Believe That Someone Is at Risk 147

Appendix F: Recommended Readings & Resources 150

Acknowledgments 154

About the Authors 155

To Order Books 156

See last page for ordering multiple copies.

IMPACT
The First Days, Weeks, and Months After a Suicide

Someone you love or know — a family member, a friend, a colleague at work — has died by suicide. And your world has been shattered. If you had no idea that this person was suicidal your shock is even greater. As you read these words your mind is reeling, your heart racing, and your body is in turmoil. Or, perhaps you are numb and confused right now, feeling detached from your body, which leaves you feeling as if you are in the middle of a nightmare from which you cannot awaken.

But it has happened – someone important to you has taken their life, and you are left to try to make sense of the death. As you grieve your loss, you may wonder if you will ever begin to pick up the pieces of your shattered life. You are beginning to realize that in an instant your life has been forever changed.

In this book, we will do our best to help you cope with this tragedy, even though right now you may be wondering if it is even possible for you to survive such a loss. In the pages that follow we will try to explain what may be happening to you right now in simple terms that make sense. Based on input from many people who have also experienced a suicide, we will give you information about what to expect and ideas on how you can help yourself. And most of all, we will try to offer you hope.

"But, how can you know there is any hope?" you may ask.

Neither of us has directly lost someone close to us to suicide. But both of us have spent most of our professional lives as psychologists working with people who are coping with significant losses. In our counseling work we have "walked" along side literally hundreds of people over the years—and many of them, like you, have lost someone to suicide. Much of the information in this book comes from what our courageous and resilient clients have shared with us. Through their heartbreaking stories we have learned a great deal about reactions to a suicide. More importantly, we have learned a number of suggestions for coping with the life-changing effects brought about by suicide.

As you begin to take in the reality of the loss of your loved one, there are three things that we want you to remember:

- **You must take care of yourself** – physically, emotionally, and spiritually - although right now you may not feel like anything matters. You have been psychologically wounded by this death, and as with any injury, you will have to focus for a while on finding ways to cope with the pain and take care of yourself. This is where this book can help.

- **You will learn to cope, but you cannot do this alone** – you will have to find ways of surviving that work for you. They will not necessarily be the same methods of coping used by other members of your family or your friendship network. That's okay. But one thing that every grieving person must do is allow other people to help them with the process. Ask yourself, "Who is the best person to talk to about this right now: another family member, a friend, a clergyperson, a therapist?" Different people can help you in different ways. Some can be there just to listen. Some can do things for you. Some will have helpful suggestions for getting additional help. But you must be willing to accept the help when it comes - what we do know is that coping with a death by suicide is too big to try to tackle all alone.

- **Even though it may not seem like it now, you will survive this** – As the days go by, it will become increasingly clear that you are likely to be forever changed by this trauma. This may well be the most difficult thing you have ever had to face in your life. We have met and worked with hundreds of people after the suicide of a loved one. These people experienced a great deal of grief; but after a lot of hard work, they also found a way to live their life and move beyond the pain. It is a tribute to the human spirit that people can and do survive this loss. And, even though it may be hard to believe right now, you can survive, too.

Let's get started with some of the first things that you may be dealing with right now.

Your Reactions

Your Body - Shock

Right now, you are likely in shock. People in shock say things such as:

- "I can't believe this is happening."
- "It seems like a bad dream—a nightmare."
- "I feel like I'm just going through the motions."
- "I feel like I'm in a fog."
- "Sometimes—for a few seconds--I forget what has happened."

Shock is a normal reaction to traumatic and overwhelming events. The human body is "wired" to respond to emergency situations with a number of physiological changes that you are probably experiencing. Your body has been flooded with stress hormones that prepare you to *"fight or flight or freeze"*. These are adaptive responses in an emergency. For example, you may feel an overwhelming urge to "attack" something, to scream, to throw something, or to explode – this is the *fight response*. Or you may feel an intense desire to mentally or even physically run away, to escape from this terrible situation, to have it just not be true. You feel like your body is "juiced up," as if you had too much caffeine in your system, with intense "nervous" energy – this is the *flight response*. Or you may just feel numb, detached, dazed and immobilized, as if you were in a nightmare, unable to move or escape – this is the *freeze response.* Other common symptoms of the trauma response include a racing heartbeat or feelings of panic, a huge knot in the pit of your stomach, or being "choked up" as if you cannot breathe, feeling dizzy, nauseous, or like you are about to faint. You also may be experiencing a disruption of your sleep or wanting to sleep all the time. Your appetite, or your bowel functions may be disrupted as well. And you are very likely to experience a great deal of fatigue and exhaustion. Even though different people respond in different ways to a traumatic event, almost everyone will have their body react in some way to this tragedy. Believe it or not, these are normal reactions when confronted with a situation that is utterly overwhelming. When it persists and gets even worse over time (which usually doesn't happen), then it can be diagnosed as post-traumatic stress disorder (PTSD).

Your Mind – Confusion, Denial, and WHY?

It is normal for your mind as well as your body to react intensely to the suicide. For most people, their thoughts go on "turbo-drive", focusing over and over again on the questions of "Is this true? Are they really dead?" and "Why did they do this? Why? Why?" and "How could this have happened?" You may find your thoughts see-sawing back and forth between "this can't be true" and "oh my God, it *is* true – what will I do?" You may even "forget" for a brief period (for example, when you first wake up in the morning), only to have the painful reality hit you once again. It is also probably very difficult for you to concentrate – you cannot read, you cannot remember, you cannot think clearly. It's as if your mind has been captured by the catastrophe, and you are unable to control or regulate it – you just keep thinking about this relentlessly. Given what has happened, this "out of control" experience is normal, but it is still very distressing. One thing we can tell you:

Even though right now it seems impossible to imagine, *it will get easier with time*. It will.

You may also find yourself having "flashbacks." Images of your loved one's body may be "seared" into your brain. Or you may find yourself struggling with questions such as

What was it like during his or her the last moments?

What was my loved one thinking and feeling?

How much did they suffer?

You keep reliving these images and questions even though you do not want to do so. These feelings and thoughts may be accompanied by a strong sense of unreality, as if this is all a nightmare from which you will soon wake up. You may even feel as if you are outside your body, watching what is happening. This is particularly likely if you witnessed the suicide or found your loved one's body. But people can form a mental picture of the death scene, even if they were not an actual eyewitness to it.

Likewise, people can keep reliving the awful moment that they received the news of the death. You may find that your thoughts focus on odd or seemingly trivial details – the sound of the person's voice who told you the news, or the expression on the doctor's face. Alternatively, you may find that you are not able to remember some of the events surrounding the death, such as who was with you when you got the news and what people said to you. You may not be able to remember these details at all.

In our work with people who are coping with a death from suicide, we are sometimes asked, *"Am I losing my mind?" The answer is "No."* This is how the mind and body react to terrible distress. All of these thoughts and reactions are part of the trauma response, and it truly is a type of *altered state of consciousness* – one where your brain processes things in a way that is very different from normal, everyday experiences. With time, these responses will most likely fade. However, if the trauma symptoms are disrupting your life too much, or if they persist for weeks and months without diminishing, then it makes sense to seek help from a mental health professional who is trained to work with people who have been traumatized (See Appendix A).

Lastly, let's return to the *"Why?" question*. Perhaps more than any other death, suicide is a mysterious, seemingly incomprehensible death. If your loved one suffered from a psychiatric disorder (depression, bipolar disorder, substance abuse, schizophrenia or eating disorder), perhaps the death was not so much of a shock. Rather, it may have been something that you feared would happen. You may have half expected it to occur. But for most people, the suicide is a great shock, something mysterious that has come like a bolt of lightning, stunning everyone in the family and community. It may seem to be so out of character with the person that you knew ("he was the last person I would ever have thought would take his life"), that your mind is returning over and over again to the question of "Why? Why? WHY???" For right now, you may be frustrated that you don't know the answer to the question. And you may never fully understand "Why?" But most survivors go through a long and complicated process of putting together the pieces of the puzzle that ultimately leaves them with at least some understanding of their loved one's state of mind, plus a hard-won acceptance of the fact that the only person who could really explain this is now gone. And they begin to realize that they will have to learn to live with the painful but unanswerable questions that still remain. If you ask people whose loved ones have died from suicide (many call themselves "suicide survivors" - a term we will use often in this book) they will tell you that, with time, the intensity of the "Why?" question subsides. We will have more to say about your need to search for answers in later sections of the book.

Your Emotions – The Roller Coaster

Most people find themselves on an "emotional roller coaster" after a suicide. You are probably going through a whole host of feelings that can change from one moment to the next. Here are some of the feelings that you may be experiencing:

- *Anxiety & panic* - Your brain is shouting to you that "this is an emergency!" Intense fear, worry, and panic are going to be experienced by almost everyone at some point, usually early on in the process, and then periodically down the road. The "flashbacks" that we just described before are driven by this same intense anxiety.

- *Numbness and shock* – in a way, this is the opposite of panic – it is as if your mind cannot even grasp what has happened, so you "shut down." Think of it as like the circuit breakers that protect the wiring in your house from overloading. Your "emotional circuit breakers" have been tripped, and so the lights have gone out and you feel like you are just stumbling around in the dark.

- *Confusion* – something that seems almost incomprehensible has happened, something that is difficult for many people to understand – a human being has taken their own life. When

6

you think about it, this flies in the face of what many of us just take for granted, which is that, "Of course, everyone wants to live as long as they can, don't they?" Sorting out the confusion, and working to understand what has happened is part of the psychological work that you will need to do. Reading this book can be a step in that direction.

- *Relief* – for some people the word "relief" seems to be an odd reaction to the death of a loved one from suicide. For some, any feeling of relief would be considered unthinkable. Yet, for others, the suicide death of a family member means that there will be no further pain in their loved one's life. It means that there will be no more calls at 3 in the morning, no more police involvement, no more arguments, and no more hospitalizations. It means that constant worry has been replaced with grief, uncertainty has given way to a final answer, a life of chaos has turned into a death where the suffering person is no longer living in anguish. If you are experiencing any of these reactions, we hope that you can see that feeling "relief" is certainly understandable. Relief is an entirely natural and human response to the end of suffering – your loved one's, and your own.

- *Helplessness* - One of the most difficult aspects of a suicide loss is the sense of helplessness it produces in survivors. You may have felt helpless to control the psychiatric, personal, or financial problems of your loved one. Perhaps you saw the suicide coming, but were powerless to stop it. Perhaps your loved one resisted all of your attempts to help. Or perhaps you didn't see it coming. Whatever the situation, you may now feel helpless in coping with your grief. For the time being, just understand that almost all survivors have these feelings at one time or another – ***and that there really are limits to how much anyone can do to prevent a suicide.***

- *Anger* – you may feel furious about what has happened - a need to blame or punish someone for the suicide. Suicide seems to release a burst of "anger energy" in individuals and families, and many people feel a need to put that anger somewhere.

7

If you feel this anger towards the person who took their life, it may be because you feel that they have betrayed you or abandoned you. Or, you may find yourself directing that anger at some other family member, at a therapist or doctor who was caring for your loved one, even at God – and, very commonly, at yourself. That anger energy that you direct at yourself can also be called guilt.

• *Guilt* – when something goes terribly wrong, human beings have a natural and powerful need to make sense of what has happened. This usually includes a need to affix blame for the bad thing that has happened. Most people, even if they are outwardly blaming someone else for the suicide, will also be privately asking themselves "Is this my fault? Why didn't I see this coming? Could I have done more to prevent it?" *This self-blaming is very, very common after a suicide.* Later on in this book, we will discuss some reasons why people tend to blame themselves so much for a suicide. Guilt is a very strong emotion - it is usually a sign of the sense of responsibility and love that you feel for your loved one. Here are some different types of guilt feelings that you may find yourself experiencing. See if any of the following relate to you:

> *Death-causation Guilt*: You feel that you did something or failed to do something that led to the suicide.

> *Role Guilt*: You blame yourself for not being a good enough parent/sibling/spouse/friend/child for your loved one.

> *"If-Only" Guilt*: You say to yourself over and over, "If only I would have _____." Or "Why didn't I _____?"

> *Moral Guilt*: You believe that you did something wrong months or years ago and you feel that this tragedy is somehow related to your wrongdoing.

> *Survival Guilt*: You don't feel entitled to any happiness in your life. You feel guilty just for being alive, when your loved one suffered and died.

Grief Guilt: You feel that you are not grieving correctly.

Unmentionable Guilt—You feel guilty for reasons that you believe are too terrible to tell, or even let yourself think about.

"Getting Better" Guilt: You feel guilty for feeling better, and for having your life move on without your loved one.

There is no simple "fix" for the guilt that you are feeling. But some facts may help you reevaluate your guilt. First, suicide is frequently associated with the presence of a psychiatric disorder, most often depression. People suffering from a severe psychiatric disorder are usually in a great deal of emotional turmoil and pain. As with physical illness, the severity of the pain intensifies the person's wish to find relief. ***Almost all suicides involve the powerful wish to find relief from emotional pain.*** It hurts to think of your loved one's emotional distress, but it is crucial to remember that there are limits to how much you or anyone else could have done to relieve their suffering. Just as no one can erase the grief that you feel right now, there were limits to what anyone could have done to fix your loved one's pain. This is particularly true if your loved one became convinced that suicide was their only option for release. Perhaps it is best to think of most suicides as an extreme alternative to continuing to live in a present state of emotional pain. Suicidal behavior is almost always born of suffering, desperation, and distorted thinking that was a result of some type of psychiatric disorder. It is an act for which you ultimately cannot be responsible. (For more on this, see Appendix B. titled "Understanding Suicide: The Perfect Storm").

Second, there are limits to how much anyone can do to stop an act of suicide. Research from people who survived suicide attempts has shown that, while many suicidal people experience feelings of ambivalence about suicide, some do not. For some, the act may even have been quite impulsive. And we know that some people manage to end their life, even while they are hospitalized on locked psychiatric units under careful supervision. In light of this fact, try to be realistic about how preventable the suicide was and how much you could have done to intervene.

Finally, even if you somehow feel that you did something that contributed to the suicide, or that you failed to prevent it, we encourage you to work towards being compassionate towards yourself. Living through the suicide of a loved one confronts all survivors with a profound sense of their own limitations. These include the limits of our abilities to help others, to alleviate their suffering, or to predict or prevent a terrible thing from happening. They also include our own imperfections and mistakes. Both you and your loved one were, after all, just human.

Some Specific Challenges

Witnessing the Suicide or Finding the Body

Perhaps you witnessed the suicide of your loved one. It is difficult to think of a more wrenching experience. The suicide may have followed an argument. Your loved one may have been intoxicated by alcohol or drugs. Or your loved one may have suffered from depression for a long time, or may have been despondent over a setback in life, and you were worried about their safety. On the other hand, your loved one may have given you absolutely no warning that he or she was having a difficult time or thinking of suicide. So the death may have been a complete and utter shock to you. And to make matters worse, you may have been the person to find your loved one's body, or perhaps seen their body before it was taken to the morgue.

If any of these things happened to you, then all of our previous descriptions about the responses to trauma are probably what you are living with now. As noted earlier, these reactions can include intrusive memories or "flashbacks" of the scene, a strong fear about being re-exposed to another trauma, avoidance of reminders of the event, trouble sleeping or concentrating, and difficulty controlling physical or emotional responses. *If you are experiencing these symptoms,*

understand that they are normal and that you are not "losing your mind." Ask your primary care physician or member of the clergy for a referral to a mental health professional who specializes in treating trauma and/or grief after a suicide, or contact a mental health clinic in your area to find such an individual (See Appendix A "When to Seek Professional Help and How to Find a Therapist" for more information).

The Police Investigation

Unfortunately, because suicide is considered an unnatural death, the police and local medical examiner or coroner are required to investigate. *Suicide is not a crime — but sometimes the police must treat the situation as a potential crime scene until they can establish that it was, in fact, a suicide.* The police investigation begins when the first officers arrive on the scene of the death, and may continue for many days. Either before or after the funeral, the police will most likely want to meet with you. All of this can add to your distress and grief.

While most police officers treat suicides with sensitivity, some do not. You should cooperate with the police in the investigation, but you (or a friend or relative) should ask them to conduct it as sensitively as possible. *Remember that neither you nor your loved one has committed a crime and you do not deserve to be treated as if you had.* If the police need to take certain items into their possession, please ask them to let you know what they are taking and when you will be able to retrieve them. You have a right to have the belongings of your loved one (including any notes or messages that they may have left) returned to you once the investigation is complete. If you need to, ask a friend or less affected family member to be a "go-between" between you and the police involved in your case. We have heard too many stories of the police treating survivors as if they were criminals, or confiscating items of tremendous emotional significance to the survivors (including suicide notes), without informing family members. *You have a right to be treated by the police (and other professionals – medical personnel, clergy, and funeral home staff) with sensitivity and kindness at this most distressing time in your life.*

11

The Hospital

If your loved one was taken to a hospital, there probably was very little in your control when you arrived. People made decisions without consulting you. Nurses, doctors, and staff people were quickly moving from patient to patient. Activity was swirling around you while you sat and waited, seemingly forever, for information. When the medical staff finally told you about your loved one, they may have been rushed or blunt in a way that added to your distress. And even if you did not discover your loved one's body, you may have experienced a trauma reaction when you viewed the body in the hospital: shock, feelings of unreality, deep anger or fear, and other intense reactions. As we have noted previously, these responses mean that your mind was trying to make sense of something that did not make any sense at all. Sometimes after contact with the police or medical professionals, people berate themselves ("Why didn't I speak up?" or "Why did I let them treat me that way?"). *Try not to be too hard on yourself* — you were in shock, and functioned to the best of your ability in a situation for which you were completely unprepared.

The People Around You

Whether you are reading this book in the hospital, at home, or somewhere else, you deserve to have supportive people around you. Ask yourself: "Who do I want to have with me right now? Who can help me cope with this?" Then ask someone to find those people. This is a time when you need others to help you with everything: driving you around, taking your phone calls, helping with household chores, and just being by your side when you need to talk. Ask people directly: "Can you do this for me?" In addition, find someone who will be willing to keep friends and relatives informed of the latest information. You also have the right to ask someone to make sure that certain people will *not* be around you if you are not ready to deal with them. Do what you feel is best for you.

Viewing the Body of Your Loved One

The office of the medical examiner or coroner is responsible for conducting an investigation, and in the case of a suicide, accident, or homicide, sometimes an autopsy. An autopsy is a surgical procedure performed on the body to determine the exact, biological cause of death. In some cases, however, the autopsy report may not specify an exact cause of death. If you are the next of kin, you have a right to ask for the autopsy report. You should be able to obtain the report once the investigation is complete.

One of the questions you will need to ask yourself is: "Do I wish to see the body?" Of course, if you found the body of your loved one, there was no element of "choice" involved. But sometimes survivors are presented with a choice by hospital or law enforcement personnel that they never could have imagined themselves having to face: "Do you want to view the body of your loved one?" Also, the police may need to ask someone in the family who knew the deceased to identify the body, although that does not necessarily have to be you – just someone who can reliably identify the body. Research with people who have chosen to view the body indicates that most survivors later feel that they made the right decision. While they may forever carry that last image in their mind, they also feel that the experience helped them cope with the understandable tendency to deny the reality of the death, and helped their mind answer the question "Did this really happen? Could this have been a mistake?" *You have every right to ask the medical or coroner's staff to give you some privacy with the body of your loved one*. Some people choose to view the body in the morgue or the hospital or even at the scene of the death - while other people wait to view it in a funeral home. And, sometimes, people decide that they just do not want to view the body at all. If you decide to view the body of your loved one, first call ahead to the morgue, hospital, or funeral home to arrange to come in. Ask the following questions:

- "What is the setting where I will view the body?"
- "Will my loved one have any visible wounds?"
- "Could you describe the condition of the body to me?"
- "Will I be able to touch my loved one?"
- "When will I be able to have the personal effects of my loved one?"

13

- "Will I be able to have some time alone with my loved one?"
- "What else should I know before I arrive?"

You should bring a friend or relative with you so they can view the body or photographs first – then you and they can determine if the sight might be too traumatic for you. In morgues, hospitals, and funeral homes, injured body parts are typically covered. If there are a large number of serious injuries, you may end up seeing only a small portion such as a hand or only a part of the face. The length of time your loved one will remain at the medical examiner's office varies from a day to several days, so call ahead to get an estimate. An autopsy may have to be performed before your loved one's body can be released to a funeral director.

If the suicide has caused significant damage to the body, the medical examiner's office may discourage you from viewing the body of your loved one on the grounds that the sight will traumatize you. *This is a legitimate concern, but the decision about whether and how much of the body to view should be one for you to ultimately make, not the medical examiner.* This is an extremely difficult moment for you, one that you will remember for the rest of your life. Take your time, and try to decide what will help you most in the long run as you face this terrible situation. Also, we have heard from survivors that, in the midst of the shock of the death, family members found themselves arguing about whether or not to see the body. It is important at this time for you and your family members to respect the decision of others. You may not understand each other's choices but it's important to be supportive of them nonetheless.

If you are reading this at some point after the death of your loved one and you decided at the time not to see the body, it is important for you to understand that, under the circumstances at that time, you made the right decision for yourself. It may be tempting now to look back and say, "Why didn't I see the body when I had the chance?" However, you were forced into a situation that few people experience in their life: seeing the body of their loved one following a suicide. Therefore, if you are feeling remorse about viewing or not viewing the body, it is important for you to find a way to let go of this regret.

Once again, you did what you thought was best for you at the time under extraordinary circumstances, for which you were unprepared.

Deciding What to Tell Other People

Another difficult decision you will face is how much to tell other people about the circumstances of the death. Although our society is changing, there is still a tremendous amount of ignorance and stigma associated with suicide. Some survivors fear that others will blame the family or friends for the death, or assume that the entire family is "crazy." As a result, some survivors decide to keep the circumstances of death a secret. Within families, people sometimes try to hide the cause of death from others (particularly children), thinking it will protect those family members from a reality that is too difficult to bear, or believing that it may cause family members themselves to contemplate suicide.

While we cannot judge what is right for you, we can tell you that *in the long run, most survivors are glad that they decided to tell the truth, and not to keep the facts a secret*. Telling the truth has several advantages. It means that you do not have to keep track of who does and doesn't know about the situation. You do not have to waste emotional energy on pretending. You also do not need to worry about people (including children in your family) hearing about the suicide from an outsider. Perhaps most importantly, if family and friends know the truth, then they can truly offer each other comfort and support about what has really happened.

The Reactions of Other People

While undoubtedly, some people will gossip or pass judgment about you and your family, many survivors are surprised at how accepting their friends and family can be. People usually want to help, but don't know how. Some may admit, "I just don't know what to say." You can respond, "You just did—you showed that you care enough to speak about it." *You can help others to help you by sharing the truth, and then telling them what you need from them*. For some survivors, just saying the word "suicide" is difficult. Today, many people are steering away from the term "committed suicide" (because it sounds like committing a crime or a sin) in favor of "she died by suicide" or "he took his life."

15

You may have some insight into the reasons for your loved one's suicide and may wish to share them with people who ask. On the other hand, your loved one's suicide may have come as a total shock. You may wonder, "What do I tell people? I don't even understand this myself." Even if your loved one suffered from a psychiatric disorder and had been suicidal in the past, you are still probably struggling to make sense of the death. It is okay to share your confusion with others, perhaps saying something like, "I just don't understand this — it's as senseless to me as it is to you." Over time, as you think it through, you may come to a better understanding of why your loved one took his or her life. It is also likely that you will come to accept that you may never fully comprehend how your loved one could have done this.

For some people in your life—friends, colleagues, acquaintances—there will be awkward moments around the topic of suicide. One example can be seen when a person says absolutely nothing about the death of your loved one, let alone the suicide. In this case, you have two choices: let the silence continue or bring up the topic yourself. There are, of course, a number of ways to bring it up. One is to say, "I don't know if you heard about the suicide of my _____. A lot of people are worried about me, but I'm getting help by _____." Another example is when you find yourself feeling like you need to take care of the other person's feelings. Most suicide survivors have found that there are times when they need to choose to put aside their feelings to support others. Your friends and family may be as shocked and upset as you, and you may feel protective of them. This is okay – to a point. But remember that the support needs to be mutual and reciprocal. Make sure you are still getting the help you need. A third example occurs when a person says something insensitive, or sometimes, downright judgmental or cruel. Should you ignore it or call them out on it? This is a choice that you will learn to make over time – is this someone that matters to me? Do I have the time and emotional energy to try to "set them straight?" Is this the time or place to do that, and am invested enough in the relationship to try to do that. These are questions that you will need to answer on a "case by case" basis. What we can suggest is that, if you do decide to challenge the way that someone is treating you, try to explain to them in as calm and matter of fact way as possible what the specific comments or behaviors are that are upsetting to you, and what it is that they could do that would be of more help to you. For example, someone might say to you, "How could they do that? This was so selfish of them." You might respond, "I understand that you are upset with them and trying to be protective of me – but it is not helpful to me when people say things like that. It would help more if you would just say that you are sorry, and let me talk about my own reactions to this." In all three of these situations, survivors have found it helpful to bring these scenarios up for discussion in a support group setting or discuss it with a counselor in order to have some practice on how to respond. Some survivors have also chosen to write letters or use the Internet to deal with the awkwardness by announcing what has happened and importantly, to explain what people can do to support them in their grief.

Dealing with the Media

Depending upon the circumstances of the death, you and your family may be the subject of media attention. It's bad enough that your loved one has died——now the TV, radio, newspaper, or Internet are involved. Many families of suicide victims say that the way the media treated them or reported the death has compounded their grief.

Remember that you are under no obligation to speak to representatives of the media. Rather, you should think about whether there is something that the media can help you accomplish, such as publicly honoring your loved one or helping others to better understand suicide. One way to protect you and your family is to designate one spokesperson from the family to deal with the media. If you want, you can even choose to speak to just one reporter. If you feel comfortable with this media representative, you might agree to grant him or her exclusive rights to the story. While choosing one reporter and one family spokesperson may not sound like a satisfactory solution, most families who have tried this approach have found it useful. When other journalists call or appear on your doorstep (yes, it happens), you can dismiss them with the statement, "Our family spokesperson is talking with only one reporter and her name and phone number is

_____." Or you can state that no one in your family is speaking to the media. This is always your right.

The Suicide Note

Some people who end their life leave a note (about 25 – 30%) - but most do not. Sometimes people ask us whether it is better or worse for the survivors to be left a note. Our usual answer is "It depends on what is in the note." If your loved one left a communication, you have probably read it over and over, looking for clues as to why he or she did this. If the message was loving and non-blaming – usually with the person blaming themselves for not being stronger or for having made too many mistakes – then the note may be helpful for you. But if the note was filled with anger – accusing you or someone else of "driving" them to suicide, the note may be quite hurtful. *Be aware that when people are acutely suicidal, they are almost always in an altered state of consciousness, and their thinking and emotions are not normal* (See the Appendix B Understanding Suicide: The Perfect Storm). For example, suicidal people sometimes believe that others will be better off without them. Or they see suicide as a way of getting revenge on someone else for a perceived humiliation or rejection. Sometimes the note is just rambling and incoherent. In other words, the content of suicide notes may or may not offer much toward answering the "Why?" question. And the content of the note reflects your loved one's state of mind *only at the time of their death*, not necessarily how they felt most of the time. If your loved one did leave a note, then you can consider it a "clue" about what was going on for them, but only one clue. There are very likely many complicating factors that led to your loved one's suicide, only some of which were they aware. For example, many people who are depressed do not fully realize how depressed they are, or how much the depression has altered their thinking. Finally, it is important to understand this critical fact: *No suicide note could ever convey all of the reasons, thoughts, and emotions that led to the final act that ended someone's life.*

When no note is left behind, survivors often yearn for a window into their loved one's intent and final thoughts. Unfortunately, when people are acutely suicidal, they often are not thinking about those around them—at least not clearly. Rather, they are focused on many other things: their pain, the problems they face, the hopelessness they feel, and the escape that they believe suicide will provide. Many people who have survived a suicide attempt report that their focus during the last moments was attending to the details of the method: for example focusing on the number of pills to take to end their pain. Leaving a note for you may have been the last thing on their mind.

(Re)Visiting the Scene of the Suicide

If the suicide took place somewhere other than in your home, you may have thought about visiting the scene. Some people have no desire to visit or revisit the place where their loved one died. It is simply a place of horror that they never want to see. Other people have mixed feelings about visiting the scene, being frightened to go to the place where their loved one died, yet feeling somehow compelled to go. And for others, visiting the scene of the death has become a challenge they feel they must overcome, or perhaps a pathway for understanding what happened and honoring the person who died. We cannot tell you whether to go, or not – only that you should give yourself the time you need to make this important decision, and to think about what your expectations are for the visit. We can tell you that for most, but not all, people who do go to the scene, the visit does provide some measure of understanding of what happened. If you are considering a visit, answer the following questions for yourself first:

- What do I know about the scene already? Has it been described to me, or have I already visited there many times before the death?
- What are my present emotional reactions when I think about going there?
- What do I expect to happen once I get there? What do I hope visiting the scene will accomplish for me?
- Are there any "risks" that could come from visiting the scene (for example, being further traumatized)?
- Are there things that I need to say or do at the scene, or rituals that I need to perform (for example: reading a letter that I have written to my loved one)?

- Once I visit the scene, how can I take care of myself so that I will be okay?

- Who should I take with me for support (for most people, it is better not to go alone)?

Some people who visit the scene consider finding a way that the place can be preserved or commemorated in memory of their loved one. Be aware that whatever you do may not be permanent. You may leave something at the scene, for example, only to later find it has been removed.

The Funeral or Memorial Service

Despite being in the depth of despair, most people want to have a funeral or memorial service for their loved one. Funerals allow everyone in the community who knew your loved one to pay respects, express grief, and comfort one another. Having some type of service will also allow you to confront the reality of the death and to receive much needed support from others. Despite this traumatic event, you must collect your thoughts and sort out the many tasks before you. Here is a list to help organize your thoughts about the funeral or memorial service.

- Who can notify family and friends? Who can help make arrangements with people from out of town?

- What tasks can be delegated? Who can keep a record of cards, letters, and contributions? Who can help write thank-you notes?

- Have I chosen a funeral home? If not, ask friends and relatives for a referral or use the Internet to choose one near you.

- Who will contact the funeral home? Who can accompany me to arrange the funeral?

- How will I pay for this? Do I want to compare costs between funeral homes?

- Do I want a funeral (body present) or memorial service (body absent)?

- Will the service be religious or non-religious?

- Prior to the funeral, do I want a private viewing of my loved one?

- For the funeral service do I want a relative or friend to create a picture video of my loved one's life? Do I want to arrange for somebody to videotape the service (for people who will not be present)?

- Are there pictures or mementos I want to display at the funeral? What songs do I want or would my loved one have wanted? Do I want flowers?

- Who will conduct the service? Are there friends or family members who want to participate in the funeral service?

- Do people wish to write notes that will be placed in the casket?

- If people wish to make donations, what organization should they designate?

- Should there be a burial, cremation, or aboveground entombment?

- If I want to put an obituary in the newspaper what should it say?

- Who will deal with reporters if they arrive?

Your Children

If you have children who are affected by this death, you are no doubt concerned about how to minimize the impact of this terrible event on them. We understand that. To read more about helping children deal with a suicide, please see the section titled "Your children," which begins on page 40.

If It Was a Friend Who Died of Suicide

The suicide of a friend brings its own set of issues. Because you are not a family member, you may find yourself being left out of things, and your grief not fully recognized. This is sometimes called *disenfranchised grief,* and it can happen both within and outside the family. It refers to the fact that many people act as if there was a "hierarchy" of who is entitled to grieve the most and receive the most attention and support. For some issues, this may make sense, such as the planning of the funeral or the distribution of belongings, which are usually decisions for the immediate family to make. On the other hand, your grief is as real as anyone else's. While outside people may focus their attention and caring on the immediate family members, you may be left to grieve on your own. Such feelings of isolation can add to your grief. If this has happened to you, find someone who can be a compassionate and empathetic listener to you. You need someone who does not assume that because this person was "only a friend," you are not entitled to grieve much. You are entitled to express your feelings and have your loss recognized as well - while respecting the support being received by the family.

As a friend, see if any of the following issues resonate with you:

- You know information, perhaps secrets, about the person who died that the family did not know. In some cases it is clear that the secret should be left to die with the person. In other cases you may be struggling with whether to tell and/or whom to tell.

- You had a special relationship with the person who died that family members do not understand. You may feel that your grief is as intense as theirs. Yet, the family and larger community do not recognize the depth of your feelings about the deceased.

- You may secretly feel responsible in some way for not letting others know what you knew or suspected—that this person was more at risk for suicide than people realized.

- You may know information about one or more family members that you feel was somehow a contributing factor to the suicide. As a result, you may feel resentful or angry at one or more people and may have a hard time being around them.

- At a more general level, you may observe family members exhibiting grief reactions and say to yourself, 'If only you knew what I know, you wouldn't feel that way.'

- The family may disapprove of you or the relationship you had with the person who died, or actively blame you for the death. They may be shutting you out of joining in the grieving rituals for the deceased, such as a funeral or memorial service.

- The family members are simply preoccupied with their own grief – and are not able to see the impact this has had on people close to but not related to the deceased.

If you are experiencing some of these issues, see if there is someone in the family with whom you could share them. Perhaps they can talk with others in the family and help them see what this loss means to you. Even if you are not able to do this, it may be helpful to find a support person, such as another friend who can be a good listener or a counselor who can help you sort out these complicated feelings. We also want you to know that while the family or community may not recognize your loss, you can still give yourself permission to acknowledge and take care of your own grief. For example, if you somehow felt unwelcome to participate in the funeral, you can still find your own ways of memorializing your loved one. Perhaps you and someone who can support you could visit the grave at another time, and you could say what you need to say at your own individual funeral for your friend. At any rate, it probably will not do you much good to keep these concerns inside. Dealing with grief is tough enough. Adding the special friendship you had with this person makes for a kaleidoscopic array of complicating factors. You are hurting. Wouldn't your friend want you to find a way to hurt a little less?

Self-Care at the Beginning

This may sound impossible, but when people ask us "What should I do now?" the answer from us is simple: "You have been injured – you need to take care of yourself." Easier said than done, right? Your preoccupation is probably with your loved one who has died by suicide and/or others in your family about whom you are concerned. This is understandable. But recall at the beginning of this book, we asked you to remember three things:

- **You must take care of yourself**
- **You will learn to cope, but you cannot do this alone**
- **You will survive this**

Well, now it's time to consider these three points in more depth.

Self-Care of Your Body

There is now mounting evidence that stressful experiences can take a serious toll on the body. *Taking care of your own body, then, is not just casual advice. It is an absolute necessity in helping you cope at this time.*

It is very likely that in the beginning, your natural body rhythms will be disrupted. That is, you may have trouble sleeping, lose your appetite (or find yourself just binge-eating), have your bowel functions disrupted, and lose your interest in sexual activity. One task, then, is to try to get your biorhythms back in order. Let's look at some helpful suggestions:

- **Food** - Try to eat regular meals, even though you may have little appetite or enjoyment of food. Also, try to eat food that reflects a healthy diet: limit salt, sugars, and saturated fats. Stay away from "binge" snacking on fried, salted foods. Instead, eat plenty of raw fruits and vegetables and whole grain breads, moderate amounts of carbohydrates, and small amounts of lean protein or dairy foods. This diet may be particularly helpful if you are having difficulty with constipation or diarrhea. It may also help to ask someone to remind you to eat.

- **Water** – Try to keep yourself hydrated by keeping a water bottle handy. Try to stay away from soft drinks and other sugary drinks.

- **Sleep** – You know that sleep is vital to your physical and psychological health. If you are like most survivors of a suicide loss, your sleep patterns have been disrupted. You may have trouble getting to sleep and find yourself unable to stop thinking about what has happened. Or, you may find yourself waking up during the middle of the night or in the early morning, and unable to get back to sleep - again because your mind will not "turn-off" enough to allow sleep to come. You may even be having nightmares about what has happened. And even when you do sleep, you may not feel rested in the morning. Usually, good sleep will return to you after a period of time, although how long that will take is very individualized. But if your sleep disruption continues for more than several weeks, and particularly if it is getting worse rather than better with time, then you need to take active steps to restore your sleep.

Perhaps the fastest way to do that is with medication that your doctor can recommend. There are also natural herbs that can help with sleep, as well as pharmaceutical medications that are specifically designed to help just with insomnia. Another choice would be anti-anxiety medications (called benzodiazepines) that can be useful in promoting sleep while also helping you to feel calmer during the day (be aware that there is a danger of becoming dependent on this class of medication, so it is not a good idea to take them for a prolonged period of time). Over the counter sleep medications (antihistamines) are not usually helpful after traumatic loss, since they are less effective and should not be used for more than a couple of days. Lastly, some of the anti-depressant medications can help you to sleep better. It is always best to take sleep medication (and any other medication or herbal remedies) under the supervision of your doctor.

For people who prefer not to use a drug to help with sleep, some "sleep hygiene" techniques may be of help. Try to go to bed and awaken in the morning on a regular schedule , and make sure your bedroom is comfortable, quiet, and a moderate temperature (not too warm—we sleep better in a cool environment). Use your bed only for sleeping, and if you cannot fall asleep after 20-30 minutes, get up and do another activity for a short period of time – do not lie awake in bed for long periods of time. If you need to use the bathroom during the night, avoid bright lights, since this signals to your brain that it's time to wake up. Lastly, limit your use of alcohol or caffeinated beverages several hours before you go to bed, and limit your use of naps during the day, so that you will be tired and ready to sleep at bedtime.

- **Exercise** – There is now abundant evidence that exercise is very valuable for almost every aspect of our being – even in bereavement. Exercise helps us to improve our mood, regulate our appetite, sleep better at night, reduce the toxic physiological effects of stress, and achieve a sense of accomplishment. Although you should check with your doctor first before beginning any exercise program, please consider adding, or resuming, a regular form of exercise to your daily regimen. Note that this does not have to be a competitive or even highly aerobic form of exercise (such as running or swimming) – just walking regularly at a reasonable pace will provide benefits. Please consider including exercise in your efforts at self-care – at least three or four times a week if possible.

Self-Care of Your Mind

Your inner emotional life may feel like a disaster that mirrors the disaster that has happened in your life. Your feelings may seem out of control and foreign. For example, you may be a generally calm and easy-going person, but now you find yourself agitated and irritable much of the time. Or you may normally be a rather controlled and reserved person who finds yourself unable to control your crying and need to tell everyone what has happened to you. Likewise, your thinking may have changed. Prior to the death, you may have been able to concentrate on a task and proceed logically to solve a problem. Now, your mind feels like it is racing from one thought to another, and you cannot focus yourself to make a decision or carry out the simplest of tasks. Although all of these reactions are normal for many survivors in the beginning, this may still seem like a frightening loss of control over your mind. Here are some things to think about in terms of taking good care of your mental health after this tragic death:

- **Trust that things will get better—they will**– Although it may seem hard to believe at this moment, you are not crazy or losing your mind. Your emotional life will eventually calm down, and your ability to think clearly and solve problems will return. Please understand that we are not saying that you will "get over it" or that you will return to your previous life. What we are saying is, based upon the hundreds of people we have met whose loved ones have died from suicide, you will find a "new normal." And equally important – your ability to feel pleasure and happiness will come back.

• **Practice Self-Soothing** – Self-soothing is a psychological term that refers to a person's ability to help themselves feel calmer, safer, and more centered – probably the opposite of what you are feeling now. How can one practice self-soothing? Think back to before the suicide - what kinds of activities helped you to feel more relaxed and at peace? Perhaps walks in the woods or on the beach; meditation or yoga; listening to lovely music; gardening; working in your workshop; exercise (yes, exercise is good for helping us calm down, as well). Try doing these activities, perhaps in small doses at first. If they help, then do more of them. If they don't, then try something else that is soothing. Self-soothing is an important skill by which survivors learn to "down-regulate" their physiological and emotional reactions to the death.

• **Find people who care** – As much as possible, it is important for you to surround yourself with people who truly care about you, are non-judgmental, and are willing to be "present" with you. It is also important to find ways to avoid or protect yourself from people who make you feel worse about your loss or yourself. We know that because of the stigma that is sometimes attached to psychiatric disorders and suicide, the people around you may respond differently to you now - and differently than if your loved one had died from a more common cause, such as cancer or a heart attack. People may press you to explain why the suicide happened, or why you didn't prevent it ("What went wrong? Didn't you know he was depressed?"). Yet right now, you may barely understand what went wrong yourself. Or you may be offered well-meaning but unhelpful explanations or comments about the death, advice on what you should do, or even glib platitudes, advice, or snap judgments, such as:

"What a selfish thing to do!"

"Get rid of all her belongings."

"Put it out of your mind."

- **Give yourself permission to reduce your interactions with people who make you feel worse.** - If you must interact with them, try to prepare yourself to put up a "psychological safety shield" by not reacting to their inappropriate behaviors. Say something to yourself like "I know this person is likely to say something that is upsetting to me. I am going to mentally be prepared for it, I am going to think of a response that I want to make, and I am not going to take it personally" You should then rehearse a specific response that you want to say to them – it can range from blunt: "That comment is not helping me feel better – could you please not say things like that to me?" to a more gentle request: "I know that you mean well, but I would rather just not talk about this now." As we noted earlier, you may want to get ideas from a support group on how to respond to comments from others.

- **Additional things to do**:

Avoid the use of excessive amounts of alcohol or drugs.

Avoid making big decisions (such as immediately moving away from your home or town).

Refrain from binging on anything that temporarily but destructively helps you "forget" or feel better (e.g. spending a lot of money on shopping, binge eating, engaging in impulsive and unprotected sex).

Try getting your routines back in place as quickly as you can. The suicide has probably thrown your life out of balance – your job is to try to get your life, including your emotions, thinking, and behavior, back on a more routine and even keel.

Self-care of Your Spirit

For many people, the suicide of a loved one raises agonizing spiritual or existential issues. These include many questions such as

- Why does suicide happen?
- I've tried to be a good person, so how could God let this happen to me?
- Is suicide a sin?
- Is my loved one in hell?
- What happens to a person after death?
- Will I ever see my loved one again?
- What good is my religion to me now?
- Who am I now?
- What is the purpose of my life?
- Why should I go on living?

These are difficult questions that you may never have thought much about before suicide came into your life. Or perhaps you have simply accepted what your religion has taught you about the answers. But now these questions may have become painful, confusing, and all too real concerns - issues that have a deeply personal meaning for you. If you have no spiritual beliefs, a few of the questions on the list may still apply.

It is not our place to offer you simple theological or philosophical answers for these questions. We can tell you, however, that the questions are quite common among suicide survivors. Suicide challenges our "assumptive world" – a term that mental health professionals use to describe all of the beliefs and assumptions that an individual has been taking for granted about themselves, other people, and their life. The suicide of your loved one may have brought all of the things that you felt certain about in your life into question, and you are now not sure of what you believe.

It helps to know that these questions are common in survivors. It also helps to talk them over with a person who can listen to your struggles without judging you—someone who is not too quick to provide "easy answers." A clergy person or a friend who can listen without having to dictate to you what you should believe may be of tremendous help. Such a person may also help you reflect on the "position" of your church or your philosophy of life on the difficult issue of suicide. In addition, talking and listening to other survivors who have struggled with the same issues, or reading books that survivors have written about these issues (see our Suggested Readings for Survivors at the end of this book), can also be valuable. *Please give yourself permission to be uncertain for a while, as you try to find the answers that seem right for you.* And know that most survivors are able to restore their spiritual and moral beliefs with time, effort, and compassionate support from others.

Review of Grief Reactions

As you face each day dealing with this terrible loss, it is important for you to try to find ways to understand what you are going through. Reading this book can be one important step. Before we move on to the next section, let's review some of the grief reactions discussed so far. We noted that shock, confusion, denial, and asking *why* are very common following a death by suicide. Next we looked at anxiety, panic, confusion, relief, helplessness, and anger. We then focused on a critical grief reaction after a suicide: guilt. This included types of guilt, the special issues of guilt around suicide, and suggestions for coping with guilt.

In this section we noted that grief reactions following a suicide are impacted by a number of issues, such as witnessing or finding the body, dealing with the police, hospital, media, and people around you, viewing the body, deciding what to tell others, the suicide note, and planning the funeral. We finished this section by focusing on self-care of your body, mind, and spirit. Let's now move to some of the issues that can take place during the first year and beyond.

ABSORBING THE BLOW
The First Year and Beyond

What to Expect as Your Grief Evolves

"The first year is the hardest – you'll be better after that." Have you heard that yet? It is offered many times to new survivors in an attempt to give them hope - and perhaps to relieve the feelings of helplessness being felt by the person who is making this statement. People often have no idea what to say, but they still feel compelled to give you some kind of "advice."

Is the advice true? Well, like most of the "advice" you will hear, it's true, except when it's not! It is definitely true that your grief will evolve, soften, and get easier. And you will be able to experience hope and happiness again in your life. One day you will likely have an experience (perhaps when you talk with someone who is a brand new survivor) where you realize "Oh! I remember feeling/thinking/ acting like that. But I don't so much anymore. I guess I've made some progress."

But this progress will probably happen more slowly and less evenly than you might hope or expect. Our society has what might be called *the "flu model" of recovery* after a loss. Think about what happens when you get the flu – you go downhill, feel terrible for a while, and then get better and better each day. And then you just go back to your life as it was before you had the flu. Many people (maybe even you) may have the expectation that recovering from the death of someone close to you will be like that. You will be uncomfortable for a relatively short while, and then you will be "back to normal." *The problem is, it just doesn't happen that way - at least for people who are deeply affected by the suicide of their loved one.*

Expect Waves or Cycles

The notion that you will get better and better, each and every day (like climbing a set of stairs straight out of a basement), is not a very helpful idea. Grieving is much more of a wave-like or cyclical

31

process, in which you keep returning to the same feelings, thoughts, and problems over and over again. Perhaps you can think of it as more like climbing a spiral staircase out of that basement, where you are simultaneously coming around to the same place, yet you're not – you are also, slowly, making your way up the staircase. There will also be many times where you find yourself several steps back down the staircase. For example, you will have periods - sometimes weeks, months, even years later - where waves of sadness, anger, anxiety, guilt, obsessive thoughts, and worry will overtake you. Some of these waves will feel almost as intense as they were right after the loss. And you may find yourself thinking "I'm not making any progress – it's been a (week, month, year?) and I'm still hurting!" If they look back at it, however, what most survivors find is that the waves are gradually diminishing - becoming briefer, less intense, more predictable, and perhaps most importantly, better managed by you.

Part of the problem is the expectation that people "get over" their grief. But we don't get over grief the way we get over the flu. Neither do we "resolve" our grief (a mental health term), if resolving it means leaving it behind us for good. ***Instead, we integrate our losses, making them a part of who we are. Grief transforms people, and profound grief can transform people profoundly.*** The expectation that you will simply get back to your "old life" and your "old self" is just not what happens when the loss is as large as a death by suicide of someone important to you. If you can make your peace with this truth - that you may never get over your loss, but you will learn to "carry" it and rebuild your life - you will have a much more realistic expectation for how your journey through grief is likely to go. And it will be a little bit easier to carry, since you won't be so focused on trying to hurry it up and get over it. ***To put this differently, you are likely to be changed by this experience*** – changed in some ways for the worse, but also changed in some ways better, as much as it seems impossible at this point in your life. Not that the death is ever good – but the changes that emerge from the loss can be profound. A member of a bereavement support group run by the first author once used a metaphor that summarizes perfectly what we have been trying to say in this section:

"People think that grieving is like having a huge boulder put on your shoulders, and that at some point, you simply put the boulder down and go on down the road. But that isn't what is happening to me. What is happening is that my back is getting stronger!"

Expect it to take longer than you want

The "one year" time expectation for mourning might well apply if you were grieving the death of your great-grandmother, who was 97 and died naturally in her sleep. In fact, such a death might have very little impact on you. And it is true that we have seen clients for whom the suicide, even of someone close to them, did not seem to have a major effect on their functioning, their life, or their identity. *So, will everyone who loses someone to suicide go through the long and difficult journey that we are addressing in this book? No – definitely not!* But for many people, this will be a very hard journey, more challenging than they realized at the beginning, or than others around them will understand. We say this not to frighten you, but to prepare you – having unrealistic and unfair expectations of yourself can only add to your distress.

It seems to us that the most important thing to ask yourself after a year or two is: *"What is the overall direction of my grief?"* If the answer to that question is "Generally better" or "a little bit better," then even if it is slow and filled with lots of "two steps forward and one step back," you are probably doing okay. If your answer is "I can't tell – about the same as I was during the first few months after the death," then you may be having more trouble than most people. It may be time to think about changing how you cope with this terrible loss, including the possibility of getting some professional help. And if your answer is "I'm getting worse and worse – things look darker and more hopeless than they did a year ago," then you really are having difficulty that will probably require help from a competent and caring caregiver, usually a mental health professional. In short, *the trend of your grief is more important than how long the process is taking.* (See Appendix A on "When to Seek Professional Help and How to Find a Therapist?" for more on this topic).

Changes in Your Relationships with Others

Your Marriage or Partnership

If your child has died by suicide, the loss of your son or daughter is likely to have an impact on your relationship with your spouse or partner – how could it not? It may draw you closer together, it may pull you apart, and most likely it will do both. Typically, couples have different styles of coping with stress, and this is equally true of the stress of bereavement. Some of these differences are probably related to gender differences. But they can also be related to an individual's personality, their previous experiences of loss and trauma, and the history of the relationship between the couple.

What we're going to say next is a generalization about gender differences in grieving that does not necessarily apply to all men and women. But the generalization is, for the most part, accurate. Men seem more likely to deal with emotional pain by processing it internally and alone. They tend to focus on how to contain and move on from the pain, and on taking action—that is **doing something**-- to reduce the pain. Women tend to do the opposite. They typically process the pain by affiliating with and confiding in other people, may need to psychologically move "towards" the grief, and may be more comfortable "sitting with" the distress, rather than trying to "fix" it. Of course these are only generalities; and there are definitely men who cope through affiliation and talking, and women who cope mostly alone and try to "fix" it. Differences in grieving style will also be found among same sex couples, so gender is not the only important factor.

The research literature is beginning to show that the healthiest forms of grieving involve finding a balance between these two "orientations" or styles of coping with grief that are often related to gender. This idea is embodied in a new model of the grieving process called the "Dual Process Model." [1] *This model suggests that in normal grief, people oscillate between a Loss Orientation and a Restoration Orientation*. When in the *Loss Orientation*, the mourning

---

1   Stroebe, M., & Schut, H. (1999). The dual process model of coping with bereavement: Rationale and description. Death Studies, 23(3), 197-224.

person moves "towards" the grief psychologically. This means the person becomes immersed in thoughts and feelings about the loss and the associated memories of the loved one. A Loss Orientation is what most people think of when they hear the words "he is grieving" or "she is feeling the loss." They may also do things that elicit the very thoughts and feelings that other people try to avoid – examples of this could include visiting the grave, looking at photographs and videos of the person, and recalling memories and telling stories about the individual who has died.

Alternating with the Loss Orientation is its opposite – the **Restoration Orientation.** Functioning within the Restoration Orientation refers to a person's ability to psychologically move away from their grief in order to focus on adapting to a permanently changed world. In a sense, it refers to what some people would call "getting on with your life." The Restoration Orientation can involve developing new behaviors, roles, and purposes in life. At times, it also involves actively avoiding the death and any thoughts or feelings associated with it - putting the grief "on the back burner," so that one's energy can be focused on coping in the world and developing new skills. For example, a woman who has lost her husband to suicide may have to put her grief aside so that she can learn new skills to get a job to support herself and her children. Or a man who has lost his wife may need to learn how to reach out to other people, when previously his wife had initiated most of the social connections in their life. In summary, during the course of a typical day, a person may think about their loved one hundreds of times and feel an entire range of grief reactions (Loss Orientation) and yet, in between those times the person may actively work to avoid reminders of the death or of the deceased, so that, for the moment, they are not immobilized by thoughts and feelings that might be overwhelming (Restoration Orientation).

As you can see, the Dual-Process Model is a "back and forth" model of mourning in which the person constantly fluctuates between feeling the grief and avoiding it in order to get on with life. This new model is an important development in the understanding of the mourning process. Note that the model suggests that ***the skills*** *involved in both the Loss and the Restoration Orientations are necessary for a person to cope – not one or the other, but both.* The Dual-Process Model is also very helpful in understanding gender and cultural differences in how people grieve. For example, most (although not all) men tend to spend more time during the day with a Restoration Orientation towards grief – "Yes, it hurts, but I just can't continue to dwell on what can't be changed – just focus on what is happening now, and try to put it behind me." In contrast, most (although not all) women start with more of a Loss Orientation – "Yes, I have things to do, but I can't help thinking about the life and death of my child – and it feels crucial for me to honor and remember the life they lived, even if it means dwelling in the pain of my grief." *The key for helping a marriage survive the loss of a child seems to involve each partner's willingness to allow their mate to grieve in their own way, while still finding common ways to acknowledge and share their experience.* The Dual-Process Model suggests, in fact, that each partner might be able to learn something valuable from the other's style of grieving, since in this model, healthy grieving involves being able to flexibly move back and forth between Loss and Restoration Orientations, finding a balance of the two. And conversely, an excess of one style, to the exclusion of the other, is often the foundation of what is sometimes called *Complicated Grief* – grieving that is maladaptive and pathological.

Special Problems in a Marriage after a Suicide Loss

- **Sex**. It is common for the desire for sex to shut down for a while as we grieve (particularly after the death of a child). It is equally common that one of the partners is ready before the other to resume their sexual relationship. As in all relationship problems, much of the solution involves communication, respect for differences, empathy for the needs of your partner, and willingness to compromise. Physical touch and holding can be enormously important as a source of comfort in mourning, and can sometimes be an adequate substitute for orgasmic sex. If the grief you are experiencing has affected your sexual relationship, you may want to find a quiet time, sit down with your partner and say, "I would like to talk about sex." Then, state your present feelings and then listen to what your partner has to say. Couples affected by a suicide report that communicating about their sexual feelings during grief was an important step in gradually regaining the closeness and intimacy they felt before the death of their loved one. Likewise, sexual activity does not have to be resumed in exactly the same way it was before the death. New forms of sexual pleasuring can be tried, and simple focusing on one or the other's sexual needs, without expecting both people to be sexually satisfied in every encounter, can help.

- **Pre-existing conflicts.** All partnered couples have issues. Some are related to on-going sources of stress in the relationship (finances, in-law relationships, parenting, job demands), and some are related to personality conflicts. Usually, couples tend to have somewhat complementary coping styles that are both a source of attraction and a source of tension as the couple tries to deal with problems. For example, when they are stressed or upset, one partner will tend to withdraw, while the other may insist on talking, even arguing, until the conflict is resolved. Since the emotional pain can be so great after a suicide death, each person is likely to use their preferred coping style to an extreme - often increasing the level of strain between the individuals. Couples also frequently expect that their partner should be able to "be there" for them in just the way that they need – but that is pretty unrealistic, given that both people are grieving the loss, often in very different ways. Sometimes (but not always), these differences occur along gender lines, with men dealing with emotional pain by withdrawing into themselves ("I don't want to talk about this – it does no good") and wives needing to engage outwardly ("What's wrong with you? Why won't you talk about this?")

Do these differences sound familiar? If so, here are some suggestions for dealing with a grieving style different from your own in the midst of a tragic death such as suicide:

1. Educate yourself. You've done just that by reading this book and understanding the tendency of one person to "lean into" their grief, talk about it, feel it, and endure the pain compared to the tendency of another person to "lean away" from the pain and seek ways to distract, to attempt to "fix," and to perform an action.

2. Switch perspectives. Try this: Stop for a moment from reading and see if you can take the perspective of the other person. Imagine for a moment that you are in that person's body and in their mind. Taking a minute or two and imagining how the other person experiences things may enable you to gain some insight into how that person is coping with the suicide. Now, come back to yourself. How did it feel? Many people who do this exercise say that it gives them an idea of how the other person seems to be feeling and thinking about the death.

3. Reduce harmful negativity. Research[2] has shown that there are five common couple reactions during a disagreement that drive couples toward divorce. The more a couple reacts with these five: *criticism, contempt, defensiveness, stonewalling,* and *belligerence*, the more likely they are to have problems that disrupt the marriage. All couples disagree and a death by suicide can challenge how couples contend with divergent perspectives. While we all may sometimes react in these five ways, research has established that the greater the intensity of these five reactions, the more likely we are headed for trouble. It follows, therefore, that the job of all couples is to find ways to minimize these reactions, particularly when the partners are feeling emotionally vulnerable. If you find that the amount and intensity of conflict between you and your partner has escalated since the suicide, it may also be time to seek help for the relationship from a competent couple's counselor, one who understands grief caused by suicide.

---

2 Gottman. J.M. & Silver, N. (1999). The Seven Principals for Making Marriage Work. NY: Random House/Three Rivers.

4. Family roles. Loss tends to disrupt people's usual way of functioning, including their family roles. For example, the person who has been the "leader" in the family may now become unable to make a decision or take charge when needed. Or the family "peace-maker" may now be irritable and combative, not patient and understanding. Even everyday functioning, such as getting the bills paid and dinner on the table, may suffer as people shut down for a while. This loss of functioning and emotional availability of family members for one another is part of what one of our clients called "the collateral damage" of the suicide. The period following a death, just when you need support from those around you, may be the time when they are emotionally unavailable as they deal with their own grief. Generally, with time and support, people are able to resume their family roles - but it is distressing for everyone to have things fall apart this way after a suicide.

5. Blame. When things go badly, human beings typically need to develop an explanation for what has happened and who is at fault. It is part of the need to restore order to our psychological "map" of the world, so that things will make sense again. Suicide may also release a burst of "anger energy." The need to understand why this person took their life often becomes entangled with a need to blame or even to punish someone for what can feel like a "wrongful death." It is interesting to note that the Latin root of the word suicide literally means "self-murder," and emotionally, it can feel like someone has killed our loved one. Think for a minute – if your loved one had been murdered intentionally by another person, how would you feel about the perpetrator – pretty angry, right? Well, suicide presents the bereaved survivor with a profound conundrum; the "perpetrator" of the "murder" is also the "victim" of the "murder." Doesn't it then make sense that for many (although not all) people, suicide can unleash the fury we might feel at a murderer, yet also the compassion and sorrow we feel for a victim – all at the same time? For some people, this anger energy needs to go towards someone other than the deceased

(e.g., another family member, a therapist, an in-law, a partner, etc.). And just as frequently, survivors direct that energy at themselves, which we believe is the basis for a lot of the intense guilt that many survivors feel ("I should have seen this coming, and done more to prevent it. How could I have been so stupid?").

Thus, survivors can feel a very complicated mix of emotions, including "mad-sad" feelings that are all fused together. Blaming is common for some people after a suicide, but it is also dangerous to family cohesion if it is excessive. We have seen families that have been permanently fractured by the blame that may ensue after a suicide. If your family is actively and intensely blaming one another, it is likely that the family will need some skilled counseling to deal with these volatile emotions and to survive the impact of the suicide. (See Appendix A for more information).

Your Children

Parents are often understandably concerned about how the harsh fact of a suicide in the family, particularly of a parent, will affect their children. They may wonder whether telling their children-- particularly young children--the truth about the death will cause more harm than good. And if they do decide to tell their children the truth, they struggle to find the words to explain what they find very hard to understand themselves – "Why did this person take their life?"

It is important to know something about the developmental processes that children experience as they grow and about how children experience the loss of a parent, sibling, or friend. Children can only grieve at their own level of maturity, so what is normal for a child at one age may not be so normal for a child who is older or younger. And of course, like adults, each child is going to be unique in how they understand death and how they cope with a significant loss.

Young Children

Depending on their age and maturity level, young children (up to ages 5 or 6) may have difficulty understanding what death means. Young children usually do not understand that death is a permanent, irreversible condition, and that the loved one's body has stopped working completely. They also have difficulty understanding that death is something that happens to everyone (and every living thing). For example, they may ask why the loved one cannot come back to life. Or they may worry about how the deceased will find food or water. Young children are likely to be less concerned with the fact that the death was a suicide, and more with the fact that the person has "disappeared." They may also be very concerned about the wellbeing of their surviving parent, sensing that the parent is very upset about the death. For young children, the death (particularly of a parent) is a serious threat to their sense of security and safety in the world. Thus, children who encounter the death of a parent are very likely to worry that their other parent may suddenly leave them as well.

To be of help to a young child, you must be patient with your children's questions, since they reflect a developmental inability to grasp the meaning of biological death. Try to give simple, honest answers to the questions, and take your lead from their responses. Expect that your young children will need to keep returning to the death, sometimes repeatedly asking the same questions or making the same comments. ***Children do mourn, but they will typically show their grief differently than adults***. These ways reflect the level at which your child is presently able to come to terms with the death. Their understanding will change as they develop through the years.

We also want to address again the important question of whether to tell your children the truth about the circumstances of the death. In an attempt to protect children, well-meaning adults may consider hiding the fact that the death was a suicide or the method by which it was carried out. But even if children do not know the facts of a situation, they are usually keenly aware of the emotional responses of the adults around them. They know something very upsetting has happened, and without knowing the facts, they tend to construct their own (often incorrect) explanation, sometimes attributing the death to something they did or did not do.

Maintaining silence or lying about the cause of death teaches children that some things are so awful they just cannot be talked about. At times, you may feel this way yourself about the suicide. But silence and deception leave children feeling alone, confused, and too ashamed or frightened to talk about what is on their mind. It also creates psychological turmoil for the child as they attempt to reconcile their feelings ("something is very wrong") with the words that are being said to them ("it's not that bad"). There is enough pain for everyone in your family right now, and communicating honestly about the suicide allows family members — including children — to be part of the mutual support that family members can give to one another.

Finally, it is worth repeating that eventually your child is likely to figure out that the death was a suicide or else hear it from someone else. When children or adults discover months or years later that a death was a suicide, they then have the additional distress of realizing that they have not been told the truth – which can feel like a betrayal and a good reason to mistrust other information they have been given by adults. For this reason, ***it is almost always better for a child to learn the truth about the death from you than from someone else.*** You can decide how many of the details to divulge by gauging your child's reactions and listening to the questions he or she asks. Most child therapists agree that it is important for a child to understand that the individual died through suicide. Your child can make better sense of this brutal fact with the help of a trusted adult. (see also the excellent book by Margo Requarth in our resource and reading list in Appendix F).

Having the Actual Conversation with your Young Child

How can you have the actual conversation with your child? Of course, there are no magic words that we can give you that will make the news not upsetting. But we can give you some suggestions about how you can reassure your child while delivering this awful news.

First, ***try to use the simplest language that you can, while also stating the truth.*** The level of the words, of course, should fit your child's general vocabulary and age level. For a younger child, you might say something like: "Something very, very sad has happened. Daddy has died." If your child is too young to understand what death means (generally, under 4 or 5), you may also need to explain what death is. "Death is when a person's body stops working altogether. That means that Daddy's body won't move any more. He won't be able to talk and to feel anything anymore."

Second, if you are religious, you can also offer an explanation that is compatible with your beliefs, such as "Daddy's spirit has left his body and gone to heaven to be with God," or something similar. These simple words are probably all that you need to start the conversation. Also, it is natural and okay for you to show your emotions in front of your child, as long as you do not appear to be completely out of control of your behavior. Showing that the expression of emotions is okay is a direct way to give your child permission to have and show their own feelings as well.

Third, once you sit down and tell your child the sad news, be silent and listen for questions. ***It is better for you to be a good listener to your child than to talk too much, or pretend to have "all the answers."*** Answer questions truthfully, as best you can. If the child asks, "How did Daddy die?" you might answer with something like "He had a sickness in his brain called depression, and this sickness made Daddy confused. He did something to make his heart stop beating. When a person does this, it is called suicide." Your child may (or may not – children will absorb the news slowly, and in pieces) then ask something like "How did Daddy make his heart stop?" or "Why did Daddy kill himself?" You might then reply: "Daddy used his gun to hurt himself, and make his heart stop." For the "Why?" question, you might say something like "the depression made Daddy feel very, very sad and discouraged. His depression got so bad that he did not believe that he could go on living anymore. But Daddy was confused and made a mistake – he should have asked for help for his depression. I want you to know that it is always okay to ask for help." Of course, these are only suggestions. Your child might not ask these exact questions, and might need to have different questions answered. Or he or she might have no questions in the beginning – but, if you show the child that it is okay to ask anything, and that they can trust you to give a simple, honest answer, then eventually they will ask the questions they need to have answered.

Fourth, a very useful principle to follow is for you to *try to understand and reflect back what you believe your child is feeling*. Some existential questions are hard for both adults and children to understand ("Why did my sister have to do this?"). But the feeling behind the questions can *always* be acknowledged and validated. So, you might say, "I'm not sure myself why she did this – I'm trying to figure it out, too. But I wish that she hadn't done this. It sounds like you feel really sad (or angry, scared, etc.) about what she did. Is that right?" If your child acknowledges that you have "read" his or her thoughts and feelings correctly, then you can validate those responses: "I know. I can understand why you feel that way – sometimes I feel that way too." The important task here is to convey to your child that you want to know how they are thinking and feeling about what has happened, and that you will accept their feelings, no matter what they are. Note that accepting a child's thoughts and feelings, no matter what, is different than accepting any and all *behavior* from the child. For example, a child can be angry at their parent for taking their life and may even express it by saying "I hate Daddy for dying" – but it is not okay to then displace the anger by hitting their little sister. A life-long task for all of us is to learn to put our feelings into words, even when the feelings are very, very strong!

Fifth, observe changes in your child's behavior. Depending on how close the child was to your loved one, and on your child's particular coping style, *you may or may not notice a distinct change in their behavior over the next few days and weeks.* Infants and preschoolers may become more whiny and unruly. They may have trouble separating from you to go to school or childcare. School age children may show increased behavior problems at home and at school. You can make some allowances in the "rules" for your child on a temporary basis, but plan on returning to the normal rules as soon as reasonably possible. For example, if your child is upset about leaving you to go to a babysitter's house, you might say something like "I can see that this is a hard time for both of us, so for today, let's skip going to Mrs. Jones' house - but you will need to start going back to be with her tomorrow. I will talk to her, so that she understands what happened." Or, you may need to be firm, and insist that while you understand how they feel, it is necessary to be separated from you. Perhaps you could offer to call in and talk to them more often than usual while they are separated from you. The point is that separations are very difficult for children (and adults) who have lost someone. Try to understand and accept that the behavior is probably a temporary reaction to the death. Just as you are not yourself right now, but will eventually find your equilibrium again, with support and patience your children will be able to do the same.

Guilt & Magical Thinking in Children

When a death occurs, especially a suicide, children are highly susceptible to guilt, just as adults are. At this point, it would be helpful to introduce a concept used by mental health professionals called *magical thinking,* which refers to the belief that, somehow, "magically" our thoughts or feelings can cause things to happen. A corollary of this is that, if something bad has happened, it must be because we had previously done something wrong. A moment's reflection will help you understand that children may blame themselves for the death/suicide. For example, a child might think "Daddy was mad at me and told me to clean up my room, but I didn't. That must be why he killed himself". Upon further reflection, you may also find that you, too, have your own magical thinking about the suicide – "If only I hadn't had that argument with him, this would never have happened." Most likely, the rational part of your mind can say "I know that is not true" – but it can still, powerfully **feel** true. *Magical thinking is something that can affect both children and adults*.

To help your child deal with their magical thinking, consider sitting down with them shortly after the suicide and stating the following as a way to help them with the guilt: "Sometimes when someone dies we may think that it is because of something we said or did—did you ever feel that way about Daddy's death?" Follow this question with silence. This will permit your child to think about what you have said and respond with an honest answer. If your child denies feeling this way, reinforce that healthy belief by saying, "Good, I'm glad to hear that. I want you to know that it is never a child's fault when a grown-up ends his or her life. In fact, Daddy's death was no one's fault." *If the child does feel guilty, gently explain that while guilt feelings are normal, the child's actions did not cause the suicide*. You may also want to acknowledge that you have similar feelings sometimes and share some of the ways that you are coping with these emotions. Encourage your child to speak with you about this issue at any time, and follow up the conversation with "check-ins" to see how your child is confronting their guilt and magical thinking as time goes by.

Other Emotions and Behavior Your Child May Show

Like adults, children may show a wide range of psychological reactions to the suicide of a sibling or parent. They may be confused about the death, and find it mysterious and frightening, wondering if someone else in the family could do such a thing. If you are their surviving parent, they may be particularly worried about you. It will be important for you to reassure them that you are not going to do the same thing as their other parent.

Children may also feel both "mad and sad" that this has happened. They may be angry that their parent or sibling has caused so much trouble in the family or hurt other people, and yet sad that they are gone, and will not be coming back. And they may feel ashamed of what their loved one has done - and not know what they should say to other children or adults about what happened. Consider how confusing it must be for a child to feel sad-angry-ashamed all at the same time. Your job is to help validate these feelings. *Find ways to encourage your son or daughter to tell you whatever their thoughts and feelings are about the death* - without judging those thoughts and feelings. Share your own thoughts and emotions, as well – not in a way that will frighten them because you seem out of control, but in a way that shows that your feelings and their feelings are normal, given what has happened. It is okay to say "I'm not sure about that, either." Or, "I feel the same way about what your sister did." This gives your child permission to express and process their feelings with you and to ask the questions that they need to ask.

Lastly, as we stated earlier, expect that young children are likely to need to ask the same question over and over. Your job is to be patient with your child and calmly answer the same questions again and again. *It is important to listen for the feeling or thought behind the question, rather than simply seeing it as an inquiry that needs a factual response.* So, when a child asks "When will Daddy come back?" you might respond with a comment that both reiterates the facts but also identifies the feelings behind the question. This might be something like "Remember, we talked about that when someone dies, their body stops working altogether, and it never can start working again? Daddy is dead now, so he cannot come back to us. But it sounds like you are missing Daddy a lot, and wish that he could come back. I understand that. I feel that way too." Or, when a child says "Why did Daddy have to do that to us?" you might say "Daddy's mind was very confused, and he made a mistake by killing himself. But you sound like you might be angry that Daddy ended his life? Is that right?" Again, the goal is to recognize what your child is feeling or thinking about the death, to validate those feelings while correcting the magical thinking, and to communicate to the child that you have heard their message about their experience.

Elementary School Age Children (6 – 12)

There is a tremendous range of responses to a suicide from children who are between the ages of 6 and 12. Of course, six and seven year olds will show many of the behaviors and thoughts that younger children do, including difficulty grasping what death means and its permanence. As children age, however, they come to realize what death is - a complete and permanent shutdown of all biological functioning of the body that cannot be reversed. They begin to show more understanding that death is universal. And, the older they are, the more likely they are to also understand that suicide means not only self-inflicted, but self-intended death - although they may be quite confused about why someone would do this. Because they have a slowly growing cognitive capacity to envision the future, older children may also be better able to understand the implications of the death - that they will have to live the rest of their life without this person. They may also emotionally sense that this will change their life forever – this is particularly true for older children who have had a parent die by suicide. They now recognize that they are different from other children – both because they have lost a parent (or another relative), and that the death was intentional. It is likely that your children will not know anyone else who has lost a family member to suicide, which can contribute to their sense of isolation.

As children move through this age period, they may also have more questions about the specifics of the death. Boys in particular may be preoccupied with the "gory details" of the method of suicide - did it hurt, was there blood, what did the body look like, etc.? *It is not an easy decision about how much detail to give children about the horrifying aspects of the death scene, but in general, the truth is still usually the best policy.* The goal is to answer your child's questions honestly, but this should be done in the least overwhelming way possible. For example, if your child wants to know the method of their parent or sibling's suicide, and what the dying process may have been like for them, you might first ask "Have you thought about that? What do you imagine it was like?" This will give you a sense of the fantasy picture they have in their mind about what happened. You may be surprised to learn that it is more gruesome than the actual facts. Combating this "worst case" version of the death is another reason to give children the facts – so they can know the truth of what happened, and can better control their imagination.

After you have stated the method, you should tell the facts in as simple and matter-of-fact a way as possible. For example, if your child has asked "What did Mom look like?" you might say something like "Mom's body was lying on the floor, beside her bed. Because she took an overdose of pills, her skin was not rosy like it usually was, but was a little bit bluish because the oxygen had stopped getting into her body. But she looked peaceful, like she was sleeping. Is that what you imagined?" If your child has more questions, then answer them simply and as matter-of-factly as you can, in your own words. Try to end the description, even if the scene was very disturbing, with something like "but Mom was dead at that point, so she was not feeling any more pain," so that your child is reminded that their loved one is no longer suffering. You may also want to add a statement such as "I'm really glad that you can ask me these questions. It is always okay to ask me whatever questions you have, and I'll answer them in the best way that I can. This is really hard for both of us, but we can get through this, and we're going to be okay. Mom would want us to do that."

The Emergence of the "Why?" Question

As a child's ability to reason develops, so does their ability to think more deeply about life and its mysteries. After a child in this age group has been exposed to something as perplexing as suicide, they will begin to wrestle with their own version of the "big" questions: "Why did this happen? Who is at fault? Why would someone do this? Could I have caused it or prevented it? Why did I respond the way that I did?" These are, of course, the same questions that you are probably asking yourself, only they may take a simpler form. For example, your 10 year old may ask "Do you think that Tim (his brother) was planning this? He told me once that he hated our family – I don't know why he said that. I guess I should I have told you what he said, but it didn't seem like a big deal then." Note that in these comments, your child is wrestling with a number of these big questions. Your response should present the same compassionate and non-judgmental response that we have suggested for younger children. Listen more than you talk, ask open-ended questions that encourage your youngster to share more ("tell me more about that") and show acceptance of whatever feelings and thoughts your child is having. It is easy to fall into the trap of not wanting your child to feel any more pain than already exists in their heart and mind. However, telling your child what to feel, "Don't be angry. You shouldn't feel guilty. Don't cry" prevents you from validating their feelings. Your job—difficult as it may be—is to encourage an honest exchange of thoughts and feelings while permitting your child to feel the pain of grief now so that he or she can begin to heal the wound. In essence, we are encouraging you to become a neutral, patient, and encouraging listener for your child's reactions to the suicide.

Religious Views of the Afterlife and Suicide

You may, or may not, have beliefs about what happens after death. Most likely those views have been influenced by what has been taught to you by the religion(s) or philosophies to which you have been exposed. And you may or may not have passed those views on to your children. It can be hard for children and adults to reconcile their loyalty to the religious teachings they hold dear and an image of their loved one now being punished for their suicide. In the past, many religions have taught that suicide is a sin, and that it results in punishment in the afterlife. *It may be helpful for you and your children to know that in contemporary times, most major religious traditions are developing a different and less judgmental view of suicide.* Part of this stems from the recognition that almost everyone who dies by suicide is experiencing a psychiatric disorder at the time of their death. (See Appendix B for more on this). As a result, it is a legitimate statement to say something like:

"Your mother died of an illness. That illness is called depression (or whatever the diagnosis may have been). A lot of the time it made your mother feel very sad and discouraged, and it affected her ability to make good decisions. It was so strong at the time she died that suicide seemed to her the only way to end her pain - that is what she thought at the time. She actually did have other options. But she was so ill with depression that she couldn't see what else she could do. And God doesn't punish someone because they have an illness like depression, just like he doesn't punish someone who dies of cancer or a heart-attack."

This is the perspective that most contemporary clergy persons are taking about suicide, and it one that may help you and your children to accept that your loved one is not being punished for that behavior.

School

School, and the peer relationships it includes, becomes increasingly important as children grow. Therefore, something that you will want to consider is how the suicide in your family affects your child's school performance and friendships. As mentioned previously, since suicide is a relatively rare event, your child may not know anyone who has lost a relative to suicide. Indeed, he or she may not even know anyone who has had a relative die, except perhaps a grandparent. This means that your child is dealing with challenges that his peers have not had to face. It is also possible that the adults at school have very little experience with children grieving a loss to suicide. So, what can you do to help your child? To put it briefly: *As best you can, you want to prepare your child for going back to school; and you want to prepare the school for the return of your child*. Let's talk about both of these.

It is common and appropriate for children to want to be with their parents when something terrible has happened, and vice versa. And it is okay for children to miss a bit of school when there is a death in the family, particularly a sudden and traumatic death such as a suicide. Having said that, it is usually a good idea to get the normal "rhythms" of a child's life back in place as quickly as possible - as long as you (and other family members) are not pretending that nothing has happened. How long is the right amount of time to keep a child out of school? The answer depends on how the child is doing, how you are doing, and the child's preferences. Certainly a few days or a week out of school is not too long, and a somewhat longer respite may be needed for some children. If it gets to be longer than this, however, you probably should consult with a child mental health professional for help in deciding when your child is ready and how to help them prepare. For both academic and social reasons, it is not a good idea for children to miss a prolonged period of school - or any of their other normal activities, such as team sports, music lessons, and play activities with other children.

When your child is ready to return to school, try to have conversations with them about the upcoming re-entry. Many children are likely to have concerns about going back, particularly in this age range. For example, your youngster may want to know what the other children know about the death and how to handle questions about the nature of the death. They may also feel ashamed or embarrassed about the suicide and worry about being teased by some children. They may also be anxious about being behind in their schoolwork and fearful that they will not be able to concentrate or catch up on their work. Or, they just may be scared about being away from you – worried that something might happen to you or them if they separate from you.

On the other side, ***work with your child's school to make a plan for their return.*** Talk with their teacher and also their principal, guidance counselor, school nurse, or school social worker about the return. Agree on a contact person at school who can touch base with your youngster when they first return – someone who your child can go to if a problem arises. Ask to have that person check in with you regularly as well, to let you know how things are going for your child. In addition, ask your son or daughter for suggestions about who at school they like and trust who could serve in this "support person" role. After asking your child how they feel about this, make a plan with the school personnel about how to explain the death to other children and how much information to give them about the nature of the death. It will help cut down on the gossip if everyone is giving the same account. Ask the school personnel about what has already been told to the children, and let your child know this information.

Also, it is a good idea to ask how your youngster can be helped to make up any missed work. If it seems appropriate and necessary, you can also inquire whether a more gradual re-entry is possible (e.g., return for half days the first few days). Usually, school personnel are very willing to help with this kind of plan and appreciate your involvement with them in working to help your child get their schoolwork back on track. Expect your youngster to have some difficulty or "symptoms" as they start back at school (stomach aches, headaches, and tiredness). Be supportive about how they feel, but be "gently firm" about the need to return to school. With the support of the adults in their life, most children are able to make the transition back to school without too much distress. In fact, for some children it is a great relief to return to the normal routines and settings that school can provide for them.

Adolescents (Ages 13 – 18)

If you have teenagers who have lost a loved one to suicide, there are some additional factors to consider. Of course, it also matters who died - adolescents who have lost a parent or sibling have many of the same challenges that younger children do and many of the suggestions we have offered can apply to them as well. However, they have the additional issues of being an adolescent in the middle of physical, psychological, and social changes that are profound. If your child has lost a friend to suicide, there are likely to be different, but nonetheless important concerns that need to be addressed. We will comment on both of these circumstances next.

Loss of a Parent, Sibling, or other Relative to Suicide

Adolescents are truly "in-between" being a child and being an adult. And so, their grief will have aspects of both childhood and adult grief. In addition to the familiar hormonal changes that are moving them into sexuality, their thinking and emotions are becoming more adult-like as well. For example, during the teenage years, young people usually fully understand that biological death is a permanent change – that it happens to everyone – that adults do not have "magical" powers to stop death (or other bad things) from happening - and yes, that people can sometimes deliberately act in a way that brings about their own death. From their own experiences of emotional pain, they may even be able to understand why someone might end their own life.

Adolescents also are working on several developmental tasks that are preparation for leaving home and beginning an independent life. So typically, adolescents become very concerned about where they fit in with their peers, both friendships and romantic relationships. They develop dreams and goals about the life they will lead when they leave home. And they often reject their parents as the source of their values, security, and identity. All of these factors will come in to play as they grieve a loss to suicide.

The first thing to remember about grief for teenagers is that, fundamentally, it is the same as the grief of adults, but with less of

53

the ability to regulate emotions and think realistically about what has happened. Research in the last decade is helping us understand that, although teenagers may have the bodies of adults, the areas of their brain that are involved in planning, organizing, making wise decisions, and regulating emotional impulses are not yet fully formed. This helps us to understand much of the dramatic behavior for which adolescents are notorious – over-reacting, acting impulsively, and not fully understanding the long-term consequences of their choices. Thus, the ways that your adolescent has been learning to control their emotions and behavior before the suicide are likely to be used in greater measure immediately after the death. For example, if your child tends to withdraw and needs to be alone when upset, you may likely see even more of that after the suicide. Or, if they need to process everything they think or feel, but mostly with their friends, not you – you can expect more of that, too. **As long as you feel confident that your child is safe (i.e. not engaging in deleterious, risky, or suicidal behavior themselves), you should respect their way of coping with the death.**

Second, **the general advice we gave earlier about being honest with your children is even more true for adolescents.** Teens are particularly sensitive to "phoniness" – in any form. Telling them a fabricated story of what has happened is very likely to backfire, because your young adult is probably going to figure out the truth of what has happened and/or hear it from someone else. When they do, you will not only have to deal with their grief, but also with their sense of "betrayal" by you. Perhaps surprisingly, your child may also have a special concern about your wellbeing. Your son or daughter may have trouble making a decision to go away to college, or to start dating, because they feel the need to stay engaged with you. This inner concern about you may not, however, show itself in ways that you would expect or wish for. It is probably not news to you that adolescents can sometimes be moody, self-centered, and difficult to be around – even when things are going well enough in their life. But now their world has fallen apart, as has yours – so you may observe your teenager being outwardly resentful and self-absorbed. But underneath this sometimes "obnoxious" behavior is almost always an anxiety about how much you have been hurt by the suicide, and what they need to do to help you (and themselves) to survive. We might add at this point, that much of the anxiety and concern of children about how their parents are dealing with the death is also true for adult children.

Third, expect that your child will have extra concerns about how the death affects their relationships with their peers. Suicide is still an unusual and stigmatized death in our society, and for many adolescents, the most important thing in the world is acceptance by their peers. Having a parent or sibling die of suicide now makes a new "label" for your child: "the kid whose parent/sibling killed themself" This is potentially a very heavy burden of "differentness" from other kids. ***Being concerned about how this will make them look with their friends is not a sign of selfishness on the part of your adolescent***. It is a sign that their life revolves around their peers right now, and from their perspective, this is one of the biggest challenges the suicide has created for them. Actually, if your young adult has made good and stable friendships with peers, and has made age-appropriate romantic relationships as well, you may be surprised at how well their friends rally around them in the face of this crisis. Try not to take personally their preference for processing this experience with their friends or their romantic partner instead of you. Your presence as a stable and still functioning parent matters tremendously to them, even if they can't articulate that right now.

Fourth, as with elementary age children, consider carefully how you can help your teen with the transition back to school. For some adolescents, the return to school may be welcomed as a "return to normal" in their life, while others may find going back to school work and peers overwhelming. And do not be surprised if, while at school, your child tends to minimize the impact of the trauma – "I'm okay, it's not that big of a deal." Again, most adolescents want to be "normal" and fit in with the peers who serve as a reference group for them. Moreover, they don't want you to worry about them, or "baby" them. This is not a sign that the loss means nothing to them – rather, it comes from the awkwardness of suddenly being so different from others and wanting to restore their life as quickly as possible. This may also be the first time that your child has dealt with death at all, so the new and strong emotions that can accompany any loss may seem quite foreign and overwhelming. Offer them reassurance and support as they cope with the tragic event. In part, you can do that by ***sharing some of your own feelings and thoughts about the suicide, without allowing yourself to make the youngster your only or most important confidant for your grief.***

Loss of a Friend or Peer to Suicide

The loss of an acquaintance, friend, or romantic partner to suicide in adolescence can result in a wide range of responses, ranging from mild distress and curiosity if the young person who died was not close to your child – to a profound experience of trauma and grief that can have a lasting impact on a young adult. Adolescents exposed to a suicide appear to be at somewhat elevated risk for depression, anxiety, PTSD, or suicidal thoughts and behaviors themselves. We know a fair amount about which adolescents are likely to have a more difficult time after the death of a peer, and we will share some of these "risk factors" with you next, so that you can try to assess how significant the loss may be for your teen.

First, obviously, the loss of a close friend to suicide can be very difficult. Of particular concern would be adolescents who were a close confidant of the deceased, particularly if they believed that the person may have intended to make a suicide attempt. As with a family member, friends may feel a great deal of guilt about the suicide, believing that they could have and should have done more to see it coming or prevent it. They can also feel stunned, angry, betrayed, and simply bereft by the death. Due to magical thinking, adolescents may also believe that a conversation or argument that they had with their friend or partner may have "caused" the suicide. Or, if they were involved with bullying (either as the bully or the recipient of bullying from the deceased), they may feel very responsible. As we noted earlier in the section on elementary school age children, asking an adolescent the following statement can help the young person sort out feelings of responsibility for the suicide: ***Sometimes when someone*** *dies we think that it is because of something we said or did—did you ever feel that way?* This can open a conversation in which you can tap into the magical thinking that often follows a death and help to separate perception from reality.

A second vulnerable group consists of young people who did not necessarily have a close relationship with the individual who died, but who are themselves depressed and struggling with their own suicidal thoughts and feelings. Children who have a history of grappling with depression, bipolar disorder, and other psychiatric problems, or children who have made previous suicide attempts themselves are more vulnerable after the suicide of a peer. There is something called a "contagion effect" among young people, in which the suicide of one teen creates imitative behavior among other young people exposed to that death. This effect appears to be more likely to happen in young people who were not necessarily psychologically close to the deceased, but who are likely to "identify" with them or their suicidal behavior as a solution to their own problems.

The third group at risk would be children who may have witnessed the suicide, or found the body – even if they had little or no relationship with the deceased. The person directly exposed to a suicide in this manner may or may not grieve so much, but they are at risk for developing nightmares and flashbacks about what they have seen – in other words, PTSD.

If you know that your child has lost a friend, romantic partner, or even just a schoolmate to suicide, please follow up with them about how they are coping with this experience. Do not be afraid to ask about their understanding of what happened, their relationship with the deceased, and how they and their friends are dealing with the loss. Empathize with and validate their reactions and listen carefully for any feelings of responsibility for the death or other painful and potentially overwhelming emotions that the suicide may have created. Offer to help your child learn more about suicide and what causes it. Encourage thinking about constructive ways to honor and memorialize their friend – things like raising funds for suicide prevention, getting involved in peer to peer counseling at their school, and other constructive ways to help educate people about preventing youth suicide. Help your child understand the profound loss that the suicide must have left on the friend's family and peers.

It is also okay to ask your child if they have ever wished they were dead or felt suicidal themselves. **Do not be afraid of this question** – this is a good opportunity for you to have this very important conversation. After discussing the question, make sure to explain that suicide is a mistake made by someone who is in deep psychological pain and believes that there is no help for them – but that is wrong. Tell your child that they can always come to you if they are feeling suicidal themselves or if they have any concerns about someone else being suicidal. Lastly, don't make this a "one-time" conversation, but instead ask from time to time how they and their friends are doing about the suicide – keep the lines of communication open about this difficult topic. Some parents have found that an effective way to bring up a difficult topic such as suicide is to do so while driving their child back from an outing with only the two of you in the car. The private and time-limited nature of the setting creates an opportunity for a brief, but meaningful interaction with your youngster. Finally, and most importantly, be aware that talking about this topic with your child (or anyone) will *not* put the idea into their head or put them at risk (a very common and very counter-productive myth). *Instead, if your child has been exposed to the suicide of someone they know or were close to – suicide has already been "modeled" for them – and your job is to help them understand what has happened and to realize that they have other options when psychological pain becomes too intense.*

Longer Term Effects of Childhood Exposure to a Suicide

Many parents are understandably concerned about not just the immediate but the longer term impact of a suicide on their child. The impact will be different for different children, depending on their relationship with the person who died, their personality, and their coping resources. Still, we can offer you a few generalizations and suggest some things to be watchful for with regards to your child's functioning.

As we stated earlier, people who have been exposed to suicidal behavior (suicide attempts of people they know) or who have lost a family member to suicide have a somewhat elevated risk of suicide themselves. However, it is difficult to know whether this increased risk of suicide in survivors is the result of shared genetics or the "role-modeling" impact of another family member taking their life - or most likely, some of both.

While the research on long-term reactions of children to a suicide shows mixed results, we can tell you that when a child or adolescent is exposed to a suicide, some will have problematic reactions such as an increase in symptoms of anxiety (worry, fearfulness, clinging behavior), depression (sad mood, lack of energy and appetite, negative thinking), anger (irritability, belligerence, fighting), and suicidal thoughts. They may also show problems in their school performance and a withdrawal from friends or family. Suicidal thinking can be manifested in many forms. Your child may show a loss of interest in the things that have normally given them pleasure and happiness. They may express unremitting yearning for the person who has died by suicide, without the gradual diminishing of that yearning that is typical in normal grief.

Adolescents may also sometimes engage in "self-injury," i.e., behavior such as cutting or burning. Young adults may also demonstrate that they no longer care what happens to them or their future by taking drugs, engaging in unsafe sexual behavior, and driving recklessly. They may show that they do not expect to have a future – for example, giving away music collections or other items or breaking up with a romantic partner. And sometimes, adolescents will overtly talk about their wish to be dead or the thought that suicide would be the "solution" to whatever emotional pain or life problems they are facing.

While some of these behaviors can be common early on after a significant loss, if any of these behaviors persist, you must take them seriously, rather than dismissing them as "teenage moodiness" or "just a phase." Talk with your child about the fluctuations that you are seeing in their mood and behavior. Ask them if they are aware of the changes, and let them know you are concerned. *And, never, never be afraid to ask your child if they are wanting to be dead or are thinking about suicide.* Asking indicates your love and concern for your child, and is an invitation to share their difficulties with you. Do not minimize their reactions, telling them that they "do not really mean" what they are saying or feeling. When these kinds of behaviors seem to be getting worse with time, rather than improving, it is time to contact a child or adolescent mental health professional who can help you evaluate your child's behavior and assess what steps you need to take to help them. Even if your child is resistant to seeing a therapist, you can consult with a clinician yourself about how to respond to and help your child.

Take Care of Yourself to Take Care of Your Child

There is a considerable amount of evidence that family functioning after a death is one of the most important variables in how well children and adolescents are able to cope with loss over the long term. Families that are able to continue to provide for the physical, social, and emotional needs of their growing children make available the sheltered "safe-harbor" that all children need to develop into psychologically healthy adults. This means everything from re-establishing the normal family routines and structure such as dinner on the table, helping with homework, celebrating birthdays, and involvement in activities, to providing the emotional encouragement and behavioral discipline that are central to healthy child development. Obviously, when one of the parents has died by suicide, this thrusts the surviving parent into the sometimes overwhelming role of being a single parent – a tough enough challenge after family separation or divorce, but an extraordinarily difficult one after the suicide of a partner. And if both parents are alive, the loss of a child in the family can deeply affect both parents and also compromise their ability to function as a parental team. Even the death of an elderly grandparent to suicide can result in decreased functionality for the adult who has lost that parent. *The consequence of all of this is that taking care of your children absolutely requires taking care of your own grief in addition to your child's.* Sometimes bereaved parents become so focused on worrying about their offspring that they forget that they must also attend to their own needs. Or they think that it is "selfish" to ever put their own requirements ahead of their children's. But to focus only on your children, to the exclusion of doing your own grief work, is actually harmful to your children. After all, in this very difficult situation, perhaps more than ever, your children need you to help them cope with this. And you simply cannot do that well if you do not also care for your legitimate needs for emotional support, rest and respite, and time to do your own grieving. ***Therefore, we encourage you to see self-care as a form of future care for your children.***

Your Friends and Work Colleagues – Social Stigma and Social Ambiguity

In addition to the "collateral damage" within a family, suicide can produce problems in relationships with your friends and work colleagues. While it is changing, ***there is still a tremendous amount of ignorance and stigma associated with suicide in our society – and this stigma spills over to the survivors.*** Many studies have shown that survivors of suicide loss are often treated differently than survivors of other types of losses. They may be assumed to have somehow contributed to the suicide or to have failed to see it coming and prevent it. This unfair prejudice is particularly true for parents who have had an adolescent or young adult die of suicide. Beyond this, there is simply a general perception that "something must be wrong" in a family that has a suicide. This overt stigma probably dates back hundreds of years in western society, when people who took their life were considered to be either insane or of weak moral character, and suicide was considered a sin by religious organizations. ***All of this is to note that suicide survivors can be shunned by some people in their communities.*** Sometimes, this can also take the form of outright condemnation from people who see the family as having "driven" the deceased to suicide. This social condemnation can happen even with people who should know better, such as clergy, funeral directors, medical professionals, and even mental health clinicians.

Even when these old prejudices are not operating, suicide creates what we call ***"social ambiguity."*** Human beings usually follow

61

unwritten, but nonetheless powerful rules of interaction in their dealings with one another. When the norms for appropriate behavior in a given social situation are unclear, it creates an awkward and uncomfortable feeling for everyone. Supporting someone who is bereaved by suicide is one of these ambiguous situations. Most of your friends and colleagues will be sympathetic to you and will want to help; but they will be at a loss as to what is the "correct" thing to say or do for you. Even though the obvious answer is that *people should do the same things they would do if your loved one had died of any other cause,* your friends may feel that the taboo around suicide makes the "rules" of proper interaction somehow different – so they avoid you, or avoid the subject of suicide when they are with you. They hold back on offering the crucial social support that is vitally necessary for you at this time in your life. Likewise, you may feel uncertain yourself about how to act and what to share with others.

What can you do? Up to a point, try to be patient with people who say or do insensitive things — they usually are trying their best. But, as we discussed earlier, also think about how you want to handle the discussion from your end, and what kind of response from others would help you the most. Remember that like you, people are trying to make sense of the death. They may expect you to be able to give an explanation for something that is still very confusing to you. Or they may say things that reflect common misconceptions about suicide in our society ("Something must have driven him to it." "She must have been crazy." "I thought only teenagers killed themselves."). People may feel they are entitled to show their anger toward your loved one, which may cause you even more pain. To head off these comments, *you may need to be assertive in telling others what is and is not of help to you in your grief.*

Also, it is crucial that you learn to avoid people who offer simplistic explanations or painful moral judgments about the suicide. *It is okay to literally protect yourself from people who make you feel worse.* For some of these people, you can simply avoid being in their company. With others with whom you must interact (family members or people at work), you may need to learn how to put up your "psychological shields" when you are with them. Prepare yourself for some of the things they will say and decide whether to "consider the source" and dismiss it, or to confront the person by clarifying that their comments are not helpful, perhaps explaining to them what they could say or do that would be more helpful. It is also okay to ask them not to discuss the topic with you further. As you regain strength, you may choose to go further, and take a bit of time to educate people who misunderstand suicide and its causes.

It is equally important that you seek out those who genuinely do want to help, even though they sometimes feel as helpless as you do. Over time, you will learn what it is that others can do to offer support and you can explain to your friends and family how to respond more compassionately. Sometimes all you need is a friend to sit beside you, hold your hand, and just be there for you. Sometimes, there are simply no words. You can say this to other people, so they will know better how to help you. Also, just so you will know, many survivors report that the death has brought new relationships into their lives that offer tremendous support and friendship. They may be other survivors, friends who have lived through some other kind of tragedy or loss of their own, or just kind and compassionate people who are able to put themselves in your shoes.

To summarize this section, you will need to help those around you understand what they can do (or not do) to be of help to you. Your openness and willingness to speak the truth about what happened will go a long way towards giving others the cues they need to understand what is "okay" and what is "off the table" in terms of discussion with you. For example, you may need to say to people who are hesitant 'It's okay to ask me about Tom – Even though it is difficult, it helps me to talk about him and what happened with his suicide." Or conversely, if you are not in a place psychologically where you want to discuss the suicide (or certain details of the death), you might say something like "I know that you mean well by asking, but that is something I would rather not talk about now." *In essence, you will have to "teach" other people about how to interact with you,* since as we have noted previously, their avoidance of you and the topic may not be out of condemnation of the suicide, but rather out of uncertainty about how to help coupled with a fear of "saying the wrong thing." If you have someone in your life who may be open to improving the support they give you, you may want to give them a copy of Appendix D: **"For Those Who Wish to Support a Survivor of Suicide"**

Lost Friendships

As time goes by, some of the people who attended the funeral may not show up in your life again. They may not understand how your life has been permanently altered and may simply expect you to get back to your old self and previous life. When your friends find out that the "old you" has changed, some will remain steadfast, but others will slip quietly out of your life. Whether consciously or not, they may see you as different--someone who has been transformed by this experience. Or they may just not know how to handle being around this issue, so they pull away. Sadly, this is part of the collateral damage the suicide can leave in its wake. Most survivors encounter this loss of support to some extent, but they also find that new people, some of whom may be survivors themselves, come into their lives. It is the consequence of undergoing the profound change in one's world brought about by suicide.

Other Issues in the First Year and Beyond

There are some other problems that may come up for you as you move through the first year, and beyond. Some of them may be concerns that you have never encountered before.

- **Holidays, Birthdays, Anniversaries** – Most people intuitively understand that the holidays, birthdays, and wedding anniversaries are going to be tough – particularly the first year. It makes sense – any time that you would normally expect to have been with your loved one, particularly in a joyous way, you are also going to feel their absence more intensely. Some people try to cope with these "remembering days" by attempting to avoid thinking about the upcoming date for as long as they can. The problem is that, when the day inevitably arrives, people who have been avoiding it are often overwhelmed. ***This is why*** *we encourage you to develop a plan for days that you know will be tough.* The plan will help you to cope better with the intensified feelings and thoughts about your loved one and the suicide. The goal is to find a way to remember and honor your loved one's life (not their suicide), and work towards doing this in a way that feels right to you and to others in your family – perhaps by doing something that your loved one would have appreciated. Here are some suggestions that you might consider to honor your loved one:

1. Send off balloons with messages to your loved one.
2. Set a place at the table for this person.
3. Light a special candle.
4. Tell stories about the person's life.
5. Sing or listen to a special song that was enjoyed by this person.
6. Create an ornament to hang on a tree or a wall.
7. Visit a special place that is associated with your loved one.
8. Write a letter to this person. Consider reading it to someone.
9. Buy your loved one a present.
10. Make the favorite meal or dessert of this person.
11. Plant a tree, a bush, a flower.
12. Create a web site to honor this person.
13. Say a special prayer.
14. Make a quilt with the clothing of your loved one.
15. Change old traditions and begin new ones.

- **The One-Year Date**– we single this out because you already know this will be a hard one. Many people view the one-year anniversary of the death as an important milestone, and indeed it is. You have made it through a year's worth of holidays, birthdays, and just ordinary days of missing your loved one. It sometimes seems as if the suicide was long ago; yet it can also feel like it just happened. While you have come out of the fog you were in right after the death, at times the pain can still seem unbearable. It is important to understand that, during the month and weeks approaching the one-year date, you may find yourself experiencing an upsurge of grief, including some of the reactions that you experienced early in the mourning process. You may also find yourself in a kind of mental countdown, vividly remembering the days that preceded the death of your loved one. All of this is sometimes referred to as an ***"anniversary reaction."*** It is quite normal, although very painful.

While many people dread the day, most people find that the anticipation of the one- year date is often worse than the actual day itself. Again, it will probably help if you plan carefully how you want to spend the day. Do you want to be alone or with other people? Which people? Are there people in your life (for example, at work) whom you should remind about the one-year date, so that they can understand what you are going through? Do you want to keep your usual routine or do you want to take the day off? How do you want to mark the day? As you can see in the many suggested ways of honoring your loved one mentioned previously, many people find that some sort of ritual can be helpful. If you plan ahead for the day, it will probably be easier for you to move through it.

Lastly, as we noted earlier, some survivors have an unrealistic expectation that passing through the one-year date will somehow make things "different." People around you may assume that by getting through a year, you will naturally be "over" your loss—or at least, much, much better. You may have harbored this expectation yourself. In all likelihood, you are now discovering that this is not the case. If your grief continues, then you are following the norm. While passing the one-year mark does prove that you are a survivor, there is nothing magical about 365 days. Your loved one will still be gone on day 366, and the hole in your life will still be there.

You will still have periods when you miss your loved one intensely and the world seems out of kilter. As we have tried to stress, *grieving is a "two steps forward, one step back" kind of experience.* Perhaps it is more like learning to live with a permanent injury than getting over the flu. You will need to be patient with and protective of yourself as you go on from here.

Finding Longer Term Support: Support Groups and Other Resources

As we have noted, suicide often changes, and sometimes ends, relationships with other people. This fact often leaves survivors feeling very isolated and alone with their grief. Even when people have a good social support network, friends and family members who want to be helpful may not understand how this kind of loss feels different. Their way of relating to you may feel "out of synch" with the pain that you are experiencing. Or, because of the judgment and stigma still associated with a suicide death, you may find yourself feeling uncomfortable talking honestly about the complexity of your thoughts and feelings about the death. For example, you may feel sadness at the loss, anger at the deceased, and relief that the ordeal is over, all at once – contradictory feelings that someone who has not lived through a suicide may find it hard to appreciate.

Many survivors therefore find it tremendously helpful to have contact with other people who are grieving the loss of someone to suicide. In fact, some research has shown that for many people, contact with other survivors is **the most helpful form of social support** they can receive after the death. Perhaps the most common form of survivor-to-survivor contact involves bereavement support groups. This could be a general bereavement support group that also includes survivors, or it might be a group specifically for people bereaved by suicide. In most cases, we recommend loss-specific groups – for example, a group just for suicide survivors. However, these may not be available in your community, and sometimes a different group might work better for you – for example, a group of all bereaved parents may fit better with what you need to discuss than a group of survivors, most of whom have not lost a child to suicide.

You can get started finding a bereavement support group in your community by checking the websites of the American Foundation for Suicide Prevention (www.afsp.org) and the American Association of Suicidology (www.suicidology.org) – both of which maintain online databases of suicide bereavement support groups around the country. You can also check with your local United Way Information Telephone Line (dial 211), or ask your doctor, clergyperson, or funeral director if they know of local groups.

What Can I Expect from a Bereavement Support Group?

Entering a support group may be a hard decision for you to make. You didn't ask for this tragedy in your life, and you may wonder, "Why do I need to attend a meeting with grieving people I don't even know?" You may come up with all sorts of reasons why you should not sit in on such a group. But if you take the chance to try a grief support group, you may find that this is the only place you will be able to talk openly about your feelings, your loved one, and the impact of the suicide on your life. Most groups in the United States use an "open" format. That is, new members can join the group at any time, and the group will consist of survivors of one month, one year, ten years, or longer. People can attend the meetings for as long as they find them helpful. Open groups are often led by other "veteran" survivors, people who have also lost someone to suicide a while ago, and are now trying to help others going through the same experience. Sometimes a mental health professional or clergyperson will also be involved in facilitating the group.

In contrast, a "closed" group format usually meets for a fixed number of sessions (usually 8 – 12), and once the group begins, new members usually are not allowed to join. Closed groups are more often led by mental health professionals, and may have a specific topic for each meeting (e.g., dealing with guilt, how to handle the holidays, etc.), and sometimes a presentation by a speaker.

Typically, the groups meet once or twice a month, and a meeting usually lasts for about two hours. Most of the time will be spent with people sharing what their experience has been like and what they have done to cope with the pain and problems that can follow a suicide. The group should be operated with a strong norm that people do not judge each other's grief, that members listen respectfully to the experiences of others, and that what is shared in the group stays in the group. Group members are most supported when they are assured they can confidentially share their feelings without judgment. You can tell your own story when ready to do so. Other than introducing yourself and who you lost, no one should pressure you to talk until you feel ready to do so. These guidelines help to make the group psychologically safe for everyone, and many survivors have reported to us that their support group is the only place where they feel free to share their thoughts and feelings about the suicide without a fear of being judged, criticized, or given unsolicited advice. Indeed, many life-long friendships have emerged from the connections shared in the context of a survivor support group.

Despite the "Hollywood" image of what goes on in support groups, people do not spend most of their time crying or baring their entire soul to a group of strangers. In fact, you may even be surprised the first time you find yourself smiling at a funny comment that someone in the group makes. Support groups are really a setting in which ordinary people can share their extraordinary journey with others who are going through the same experience – and that means all aspects of their experience, even the funny things.

One suggestion: do not decide whether you will continue coming until you have attended two or three meetings. It is common to awaken the next day after the first meeting with, as some people describe it, an "emotional hangover." You have done some hard but necessary work. Give the group a chance before you decide whether it is going to be of help to you or not.

Other Types of Survivor-to-Survivor Contact

Face-to-face bereavement support groups are not the only way to find solace through contact with other survivors. The Internet provides survivors with the ability to "meet" and chat with survivors from around the world. There are bulletin boards where survivors can read and respond to the stories of other survivors and also post their own stories when ready. There are even online chat groups where people gather at the same time each week to exchange messages with one another in "real time." Another important development is the growth of survivor outreach teams, where trained volunteer survivors meet with new survivors (individuals or families) in person, usually at the survivor's home. It can be enormously helpful to be visited soon after the death by other caring survivors who have lived through the same excruciating experience – they can offer information, referral to resources, and hope for the ability to survive. The American Foundation for Suicide Prevention is now offering this type of outreach service through many of its local chapters around the U.S. (see www.afsp.org/SOP).

SURVIVING:
Learning to Live with Your Loss Over Time

Into the Second Year and Beyond

Okay - you have survived the first year or two. What can you expect now? Well, learning to live with your loss should gradually become more familiar, a bit softer, not quite so much a "24/7" kind of thing. Your biological functioning should be returned to a more or less stable and livable level. You can sleep better now, your appetite is back, and the headaches or stomach upset that were so distressing in the beginning have probably decreased. Likewise, the sense of shock, panic, and despair should, for the most part, be receding. In short, the trend of your grief should be gradually improving, with the kind of "two steps forward, one step backward" motion that we described previously. *Please note that we are not saying that you should be "over" your grief. Make no mistake about it – there will be days when things feel as bad as they did in the beginning.* Keep in mind that most (although not all) suicides are a surprise to people, and the psychological numbing that goes along with being stunned by the death is actually a kind of "emotional anesthesia." People often do not feel the full brunt of the loss at the very beginning because of the protective effect of this psychological shock. When that starts to wear off, the pain can sometimes be worse. In essence, as the many months have come and gone, you are realizing on a fuller and more profound level the truth of what has happened and what this loss means to you. It is, in short, becoming more psychologically real.

But what if the trend of your grief seems to be not up, but "flat', or perhaps even down? What if each day seems to be harder than the one before, and your hope about feeling better is the thing that is receding? We have some thoughts on this that we will share here, and you can also take a look at Appendix A **"When to Seek Professional Help & How to Find a Therapist."** First, we want to note that there is some research now that suggests that for some people, it can get worse in some ways in the second and third years.

71

For example, for bereaved parents, suicide can feel like such a failure in one's job as a mother or father to protect your child from all harm. Even when your mind knows that it is simply impossible to protect your children from everything that might happen (including mental illness), your heart still wants to believe that if only you were a good enough parent, you would have been able to keep your son or daughter safe. The suicide of a child is a blunt, harsh realization that things can happen to our children that are ultimately out of our control. And the sense of failure, guilt, and unworthiness that most parents feel can sometimes go on for quite a long time. This is probably why some parents have a rougher second and sometimes even third year than they do the first – the "shock" has worn off, but the self-evaluation and recrimination have not. And of course, your ache to be with your child again is still intense. Sometimes, other bereaved individuals can have a similar kind of intensification of their grief after the first year.

Depression & Grief

Perhaps it would be useful to say something here about **the difference between grief and depression.** The field of grief studies has debated for a long time about what the similarities and differences are between grief and depression. This is so because, in the beginning, the two are pretty much the same, and difficult to distinguish. Both involve a loss of energy, strong feelings of sadness, dysregulation of a person's bio-rhythms (sleep, appetite, etc.), a loss of the ability to feel pleasure or enjoyment in one's life, and in severe cases, feelings of hopelessness that can include thoughts of suicide. As time goes by, however, the differences become clearer.

One thing that seems to distinguish depression from grief over time is the powerful feeling of **unworthiness** that depressed people can experience. This is unlike grief, where an individual strongly yearns to have their loved one back, but usually does not feel like a bad or unworthy person because of the death. Of course, this is complicated after suicide, since almost all survivors feel at least some guilt or remorse after the death. But in a full-blown depression those feelings of unworthiness can become overwhelmingly strong, and the feelings of very low self-esteem seem like the absolute "truth", rather than just an unfair or irrational feeling.

A second distinction between depression and grief is in their variability. When people are depressed, the negative mood and thoughts tend to be more or less constant. With grief the process is more cyclical or wave like—as time goes on the bereaved person does not consistently experience low mood, but rather intermittent waves of sadness and other grief-related emotions sweeping over them. Over time, our ability to begin to enjoy ourselves, to look forward to things, and to be engaged with life gradually returns. With sufficient time, grieving people begin to have good days that may still sometimes be punctuated by bad days. The things that previously provided pleasure and meaning in life start to provide these feelings again – fleetingly at first, and then gradually for longer periods of time. In contrast, people who are depressed do not tend to have this gradually improving trend in their mood, and instead, feel more or less constantly in a low mood.

Lastly, the feelings of hopelessness and thoughts of suicide are different for people who are grieving, and people who are depressed. It is not uncommon for people bereaved by suicide to have thoughts like "I don't care if I live anymore" and "I don't know if I can go on" – something that mental health professionals call *passive suicidal ideation*. It reflects a temporarily lowered investment in staying alive, because life is so painful right now and ability to feel pleasure is missing. In contrast, people who are truly depressed may display *active suicidal ideation* – not only a loss of interest in life, but also an active wish to be dead. People who are clinically depressed may become preoccupied with the idea of suicide, and how they can end their life. They may also begin taking steps to act on these thoughts, such as purchasing a firearm, closing down their affairs and relationships with other people, and even rehearsing the suicide (taking a small overdose of pills or putting a rope around their neck to see if they have the "courage" to carry out the act). All of these behaviors are reflective of someone who is seriously depressed, and at much greater risk for suicide. They are not characteristic of normal grief, even grief after a suicide. *If you find yourself experiencing more and more symptoms of a true clinical depression (strong feelings of unworthiness, a persistently low mood, and an active wish to be dead), then it is definitely time to seek help from a competent mental health professional who understands depression in the context of bereavement.* Again, please refer to Appendix A, **"When to Seek Professional Help & How to Find a Therapist"**.

Suicidality in Survivors: Are You at Risk for Suicide Now?

This is an anxiety-filled question – one that we have been asked many times by survivors. We discussed this earlier in the section on children, but it bears revisiting. ***The short answer is "Yes – but only by a little bit."*** The longer answer requires a more complicated explanation of risk, and what it means for you. First, it is quite natural that you might be concerned about this issue. When any kind of trauma happens in our life, we wonder "can it happen again?" It has been understood for a long time that people who die by suicide are more likely to have been exposed to the suicide of someone else in their life.

So, if you and your loved ones have lost someone to suicide, should you be worried about suicidality in yourself, or in others who are close to you? Our answer is: ***You should be more vigilant, but not terrified.*** Given the somewhat elevated risk in most survivors, it makes good sense that you educate yourself and others in your family about psychiatric disorders and the risk for suicide. We think that it is a good idea, in particular, to educate children about suicide and psychiatric disorders after they have lost a parent, sibling, or close friend to suicide, so that they can recognize if they are showing the signs of being depressed - and will be more comfortable getting help for themselves. This is another powerful reason why telling children the truth about the suicide of a loved one is a difficult, but necessary thing to do. Likewise, if you are a survivor and find yourself thinking about suicide, you should first understand that you are not abnormal, and this is not uncommon. What it does mean, however, is that if your thoughts of suicide are becoming stronger with time, you should definitely seek competent mental health assistance to deal with your distress. Again, you should be vigilant, but not terrified. For more information about seeking professional help and risk of suicide, see Appendices A & E "**When to Seek Professional Help & How to Find a Therapist**" and "**If You Are Concerned About Someone Being Suicidal**".

Your World View is Changing

When a tragedy occurs in a person's life, their outlook on life may be permanently altered. It is as if the foundation of your life has been destroyed, like an earthquake can destroy your house in an instant. A suicide can undermine your sense of trust in others and your belief in your own competence, self-worth, and mastery over your life. After such a tragedy, the universe itself may no longer seem benevolent. A central task for you as a survivor is to rebuild your sense of safety, control, order, and goodness in the world. For some, suicide produces a crisis of faith: "How could God let this happen?" For others, it raises profound questions about life, death, and the purpose of living: "What do I believe about life after death?" "What is the point of my life?" For almost all survivors, it produces a sense of having been injured by life, a realization that others whom you love can nonetheless do things that break your heart and wound your soul.

Yet unlikely as it may seem, you may also find that the struggle to cope with a loved one's suicide is producing psychological and spiritual growth within you. Some individuals report that, over time, they have noticed positive changes in their outlook on life. They have come to understand that life is precious and without guarantees. They have learned "not to sweat the small stuff." Their values and priorities have shifted. Some feel a deeper sense of connection to something larger than themselves, whether it takes the form of God, or Spirit, or their fellow human beings. Many vow not to put off important activities, such as taking time to be with loved ones, mending broken relationships, or expressing love to others. Because they understand what it means to feel confused, helpless, and alone, many survivors also develop a more compassionate understanding of the pain of other people. Having confronted the brutal fact that some people end their lives, many survivors become clearer about their own reasons to go on living. ***All of these changes have a name in the mental health field: Post Traumatic Growth***. It is a real phenomenon that many survivors will experience. We are not suggesting that survivors welcome the suicide. Nor are we saying that the suicide was "supposed to happen" or that "everything happens for a reason" (although sometimes survivors come to that conclusion). Instead, we are saying that, in a way that can feel surprising and mysterious--yet none the less real--survivors may find new and deeper meanings in their life after the suicide of their loved one. We know that you will always miss your loved one, and to some extent the pain will always be there. But in spite of the suicide, you may find yourself growing and changing – often in ways that you could never have imagined before this tragedy occurred. We will have more to say about this next.

"Don't Waste Your Grief!" – Post Traumatic Growth

We once heard a psychiatrist who has spent most of his career working with suicidal patients speak to an audience of suicide survivors. A bereaved mother in the audience got up and asked the doctor "What am I supposed to do with my life now that my child has died? I am completely lost." Without a moment's hesitation, the doctor answered "Well, don't waste your grief." What a remarkable piece of advice! What he was saying was "despite this tragedy, there is an opportunity to make something redemptive come out of it - something that honors the life of your loved one and makes you a better person." As we noted earlier, this phenomenon is called ***Post Traumatic Growth***, and it can be seen in the positive changes that may emerge from great suffering and tragedy. Please understand, we are not saying that the suicide of your loved one will ever be a good thing. But, because we have known so many people who have walked this painful journey and have managed to make something good come from what they have endured, we know that this can happen.

What does Post Traumatic Growth look like? Well, it can take many forms, and there is surely no single path that all survivors follow in growing after such a loss. Some people find a new purpose or mission in their life and become outright activists. They dedicate energy, money, and/or their precious time to help prevent suicide in their communities and to reach out to new survivors going through the same ordeal. They may volunteer with a suicide prevention organization in their community, or help an organization like the American Foundation for Suicide Prevention raise funds for its research and survivor activities.

Other people do not become politically active, but work at becoming a better person – kinder, more compassionate, and more loving towards other people. They may pay more attention to relationships that have been neglected and try to become a better partner, parent, or friend. And still others will work on a specific problem or issue in their life that they have avoided. For example, a parent might feel deep guilt because their drinking problem contributed to their lack of awareness of their adolescent's depression and drug usage. After the tragic death of their child to suicide, they may vow to become "clean and sober" and to confront their alcohol abuse and its consequences. In effect, they vow to make their child's death not be in vain by dealing with their own life problem. Sometimes, particularly after a suicide, Post Traumatic Growth involves a form of "atonement" or as they say in Alcoholics Anonymous, "making amends." This means that survivors take the guilt they feel for "mistakes of omission or commission," and work to make something healing come from their actions now. They channel the energy of their grief into being of service to others, and to making the world a little better place. It is both a contribution to the world, and is healing for the survivor.

Lastly, many survivors will experience Post Traumatic Growth in the form of a changed outlook on life. Their sense of perspective and priorities about what is really important in life is changed. This includes their ways of looking at relationships with others, the value of expressing love more freely, and the joy of being of service to other people. They may put more time and emphasis on relationships rather than pursuing money, power, or status. They may have a new and deeper awareness of the brevity and uncertainty of life, and undertake to live each day mindfully and to the fullest. And their feelings about death, including their own mortality, may change. Death may no longer be as frightening or taboo, and their spiritual faith and readiness to "accept life on its own terms" may grow. These are just some of the many ways that survivors we have known have grown psychologically and spiritually after the loss of their loved one to suicide. Many months and years down the road, you too may find that you have changed – in unexpected and remarkable ways.

Coping Over the Longer Term

If you are reading this section, you may be well into your second year or beyond. Or perhaps you are new in your grief and looking for hope that you can rebuild your life down the road. Well, you can. We have seen this happen so many times with survivors that we know it is possible. But what does getting better look like over the longer term? You may have heard people talking about "healing" from their loss. But, what does it even mean to heal?

Perhaps we can begin by saying what healing is not, rather than what it is. Recall that that grief is not really something that people "get over" like a person gets over the flu. Rather, grieving is a transformational process that usually changes people – their behavior, their feelings, their values, and their outlook on life. So, the goal of grieving is not so much to "get back to normal" or "back to your old self." Rather, it is to find a "new normal" that acknowledges what has happened, but finds that life can still hold meaning, purpose, and pleasure. Our preference is to use the word "integration" – people learn to integrate this profound loss into who they are and what their life story means. To use the "boulder" metaphor that we presented earlier, recovery after a traumatic loss is about learning to carry this boulder better, rather than putting it down and leaving it behind. Also, to get better does not mean you have somehow forgotten your loved one. Long-term survivors tell us that, while they do move on with life in the context of their "new normal," they carry their loved one with them - *always*.

Continuing Bonds in Bereavement

"Death ends a life, not a relationship" – Mitch Albom – "Tuesdays with Morrie"

For quite some time, mental health professionals have propagated a widely-held but mostly unhelpful notion that the endpoint of grieving is to withdraw emotional energy from the relationship with the deceased person. It has been believed that people who failed to withdraw that energy had something called "unresolved grief." The problem with this idea is that it just doesn't fit with the lived experience of many, if not most, people who are mourning a loss. In recent years the mental health profession has begun to realize that most people, for much of human history, have believed in some form of connection with their dead. So what is the nature of this connection with deceased dead loved ones after they are gone?

It is not our place to judge the beliefs that people have about the afterlife. Most of the major world religions offer a vision of some kind of continuation of the spirit, soul, or consciousness after death. Many religions suggest that people who have lived a moral life will go to a place of unsurpassed peace and beauty. For some people, these beliefs form the bedrock of their religious faith. Other people do not believe that there is any form of continuation of the person who has died – death is the complete cessation of that individual and their consciousness forever. And still others are unsure, or unconcerned with the question of life after death.

What is clear is that our loved ones do live on - in our memories of them. And because of this, people can continue to use the relationship with the deceased in some of the ways that they did when the person was alive – as a source of emotional support and comfort, as an inspiration for their own life, even as a companion who journeys forward with them through the rest of their life. We believe that for many people, this idea of a "continuing bond" with the dead can be a very constructive thing – if it meets two criteria. The first is that you are not psychologically pretending that the biological death has not happened. It is true that a certain amount of avoidance of the reality of death is quite common, even necessary, in the beginning of the mourning process. But over time this avoidance should subside, as the fact of biological death becomes psychological reality. When people need to rigidly pretend to themselves and others that the person has not died, this is usually a clear indication of a very difficult time coping with the loss. Such an extreme form of denial calls for professional help in dealing with the truth.

The second criteria about continuing bonds is that, with sufficient time, you should be able to psychologically reinvest in your own life, and not be "possessed" by thoughts and feelings about your loved one and their death. Please note that reinvesting in life does **not** mean that you have to replace or forget about your loved one. No one can replace your loved one. But reinvesting does mean that you become actively engaged in your life again in a manner that provides meaning and pleasure for you – not just grief. For example, a woman who loses her husband may decide not to remarry. But after a period of mourning, she would probably become reinvested in her relationships with her children and grandchildren, or her work, her friends, and her church – rather than simply staying a "widow in mourning" for the rest of her life.

Continuing Bonds After Suicide

The nature of a continuing bond with a loved one is often more complicated and troubled after a suicide, for a couple of reasons. As we have described previously, suicide itself almost always involves a kind of rupturing of the relationship. It can be experienced as a betrayal, an abandonment, or even an act of revenge or punishment by the deceased. Whether you were an eyewitness to the death scene or not, the violent nature of the suicide may "taint" what would otherwise be good memories of your loved one with mental memories of the sights and sounds of the final minutes of their life.

Second, it is not uncommon that, leading up to the suicide, the relationship with the deceased was filled with conflict, substance abuse, even violence. Perhaps you were considering whether you needed to distance yourself from, or even end the relationship with your loved one because of the problems they were having. In other words, you may have had many ambivalent feelings about your relationship with the deceased person. Perhaps you had already withdrawn from them. After their suicide, part of you may be grieving their death; yet, as we noted earlier, you may also feel relieved or even liberated by their death. In this case, you may not wish to continue an on-going psychological relationship with the deceased. You may want to do everything you can to forget the person and your life with them. This is your right, and we cannot judge your decision. What we can tell you is something that you already know: it is usually difficult for people to simply forget about someone who has been psychologically important in their life, even if many of the memories are painful. As we stated a few pages back, what you can do is decide what aspects of the person or the relationship you wish to focus on and honor – and those which you wish to leave behind you. Suicide is not the only important thing about this person's life – and usually there are positive moments and memories about the course of the individual's life that you may want to remember. It is okay to concentrate on these "good" memories, and leave the others behind.

Feeling (or Not Feeling) the Presence of Your Loved One

Some people report that they feel the presence of their loved one after the death. Some feel it constantly while others experience it only once in a while. Survivors sometimes report dreams, visions, sounds, or other sensations that convince them that they are in the presence of the deceased person. These reports are not unusual, although they are by no means universal. If this has happened to you, then your task is to decide what the experiences mean for you. If you are concerned about these events, talk to a counselor knowledgeable about grief. We do want you to know that having these experiences does not mean that you are "losing your mind", or that you are abnormal.

Survivors who have not had such experiences sometimes wonder why they have been "left out," perceiving it as a further rejection from their loved one. It is not clear why some people have this experience and others do not, and we would not presume to try to explain this phenomenon. We can tell you that while most survivors do not report such occurrences, a significant minority do. The presence or absence of seemingly supernatural experiences is not a measure of the love you had for your loved one, or they for you. Regardless of whether you have had this type of experience or not, you can develop a continuing psychological bond with your loved one by cultivating recollections, sharing stories, and keeping your loved one's memory with you as you go forward.

Suicide and Your Spirituality

We are not clergymen, and we are not in a position to directly counsel people about their questions and concerns as they relate to their particular religious tradition. But we do know that the suicide of a loved one can produce a kind of "spiritual crisis" for many survivors. For some, the question "Where is my loved one now?" moves from being just an abstract theological issue about the afterlife to an intensely important question about the well-being of their beloved's soul. For survivors from some faith traditions, the specific questions of heaven, hell, afterlife and punishment for the suicide can be agonizing problems. We can tell you that although almost all of the world's major religions oppose suicide, the belief that the deceased is condemned by God for their actions is changing rapidly. It is being replaced by a much more compassionate and forgiving perspective on how God views suicide – as the final, desperate act of a tormented person who was suffering from a psychiatric illness. Many clergy are now teaching that God does not punish people because they suffered from an illness – instead, God feels great compassion for their suffering, and welcomes them home after their death.

This crisis of faith can take a different form for other survivors. Rather than worrying about whether their loved one is being punished by God, some survivors may feel angry or betrayed by God. How could God allow this to happen when you and the deceased individual have been good people, and have tried your best to adhere to the rules that God has laid out? Or, you wonder if the suicide is some kind of punishment from God for mistakes that you have made. For some, it is hard not to think this way after a suicide. But most clergy today recognize that suicide is not someone else's fault, and it may not even be the fault of the person who took their life. After all, if we accept that suicide is closely connected with psychiatric illness, and that people can die of these illnesses - in the same way that they can die of cancer or heart disease - then the suicide/illness is not really anyone's fault. It is, instead, the result of a complex process that we do not fully understand, but which science is moving closer to eventually unraveling and preventing. So while we may feel anger at losing our loved one, it should really be no different than the anger we might feel if someone died of cancer or a stroke.

We have also known people whose spiritual issues arose not so much with God, but with their faith community. As in the rest of society, survivors can be avoided and sometimes even condemned by people in their church. Most of this avoidance does not usually take the form of outright disapproval, but rather what we call *social ambiguity* – the awkwardness that people feel around psychiatric disorder and suicide, and their discomfort about what to say or do around a survivor. If you have encountered this within your congregation, try to remember that people in church--including members of the clergy--are just fallible human beings, too. They make mistakes and don't always act with the best of thoughtfulness and compassion. You may need to do some education of your fellow church members about what causes suicide, and what they can do to be of help to you. (See Appendix D **"For Those Who Wish to Support a Survivor of Suicide Loss."**) By the way, don't assume that just because a clergyperson has been to seminary that they have been well trained in how to help someone who is mourning a suicide loss – unfortunately, far too many religious educational programs leave out grief and bereavement, including suicide bereavement, from their curriculum. As with all the folks with whom you interact, protect yourself from the people who are downright judgmental and hurtful, and be patient and direct with those who are trying their best to help. Most people want to support you, but do not know how – and you will sometimes have to be their teacher about what you need from them.

To summarize this section, we understand that suicide can be a genuine crisis of faith for many survivors – one where they feel unprotected by God, worried about the soul of their loved one, and misunderstood by their fellow worshipers. For all of these reasons, survivors can be left feeling profoundly alone with their grief. If this happens to you, we encourage you to take good care of your "spiritual self" and to think about what you need to do to protect and take good care of your whole self. If the problem is with God, perhaps prayer and talking "heart to heart" with God and your clergyperson can be of help. If, on the other hand, the problem is with your congregation or clergyperson, perhaps you want to do some reading about what others in your religious tradition have said about suicide, or look at joining another congregation that is less judgmental. We know that this crisis can only add to the pain of losing someone to suicide – yet like other aspects of this experience, we have also seen it add to the depth of faith and trust that survivors are able to develop over time, as they weather this most difficult of life experiences with God's help.

Atheism or Agnosticism

If belief in a higher being or spirits is not where you are in life and/or you do not have any particular religious beliefs about life after death, then you may be feeling a true sense of finality. There is no anticipation that you will see your loved one again, which is painful. On the other hand, there is no judgment about suicide from a spiritual perspective, or worry that your loved one is being punished. For some atheists or agnostics, there is comfort in the belief that their loved one is at peace and free from any form of suffering.

Learning to Carry the Loss Going Forward

What are some of the signs that one is integrating the loss and on a journey towards a new normal? While they will differ somewhat for each individual, here are some of the changes that we have noticed in our clients who have made great progress:

- **Return of your functioning** – over time, your ability to function in your life roles – as a worker, as a family member, as a friend – has been returning. This is the usual course of bereavement – the disruption and dysregulation that are characteristic of early grief after a suicide can be very intense. But with time, support, and effort, these "symptoms" typically subside, and an individual's capacity to function returns. Sometimes, this reappearance of functioning "regresses," and we lose some of our progress for a while – a common occurrence around the anniversary of the death, or the holidays. But, as you move beyond the second year, the general trend is "up" and you should be gradually feeling better.

- **Involuntary to voluntary** – right after the death, your experience of your grief was probably mostly "involuntary." By that, we mean that the waves of sorrow, anger, panic, etc. seemed out of control. Put differently, your grief was in control of you. For example, you may have found yourself breaking down and crying at unexpected and unwanted times – perhaps at work, or while you were out with friends for a social evening. Over time, you may have noticed that your grief has become more "voluntary." You probably are becoming much more skilled at choosing when you allow yourself to react to your loss, and when you choose to avoid it. *We call this acquired ability "learning to dose oneself;" and it is a good skill, one that helps people feel more normal and in control of themselves.* This is likely one of the abilities that have been growing as your journey progresses.

- **Changes in remembering** - In the beginning, remembering your loved one was decidedly a double-edged sword. You wanted to remember them and to use those memories to hold on to them. But every time you found yourself remembering, it also hurt tremendously. It confronted you with the painful truth that your loved one was now gone. With time, remembering slowly moves from being a painful confrontation with the death to being a great treasure – a chance to go back and recall the sweet and wonderful things about your loved one – to "visit" with them again. This is why we encourage our clients, when they are ready, to cultivate memories of their loved one. Looking at photographs, watching videos, writing down memories, telling and listening to stories about your loved one – all of these can be helpful ways of developing a "continuing bond" with them.

- **A whole life** - If your relationship with this person was contentious, it may be easy to focus on those bad times in your life. However, your job now, as you move on with your life is to concentrate on the good memories, the ones that bring you joy and help you to let go of the painful ones. This can be particularly important in suicide, where the manner of death usually creates painful memories all by itself. *It is important to remember that your loved one had a life before the suicide (and before they were depressed) that deserves to be remembered.* Suicide was the last event in your loved one's entire life - but remembering the joys and sorrows, the triumphs and setbacks of their life, in all their completeness, is much more important than concentrating on the last few days or weeks of their life. In short, one of the most important goals of your grief journey is to arrive at a point where you can remember the life of your loved one without dwelling on the manner in which they died.

- **The return of pleasure** – Like depression, grief can rob us of our ability to experience pleasure in our life. By pleasure we mean everything from the physical enjoyment of our bodies (good food, sex, etc.) to the social happiness of being with those we love, to the spiritual joy of finding meaning and purpose in our lives. With time and griefwork, the ability to experience pleasure begins to return. Sometimes, after a death like suicide, people feel guilty about experiencing pleasure again. You may ask yourself "how could I be feeling pleasure when my loved one has died?" We understand this feeling – it is a kind of loyalty to this person, or perhaps even a way of "doing penance" for the death. *But we encourage you to allow the return of joy and delight into your life.* The return of happiness is <u>not</u> a measure of whether you loved this person, or continue to grieve their death. In fact, if your loved one was able to come back and have a conversation with you, isn't it likely that they would say something like "I don't want you to suffer any longer. This was not your fault, and I do not want my death to burden you for the rest of your life. Please find happiness again, and do this to honor me."

- **The return of a future orientation** – when a loved one dies, we tend to focus on our past relationship with the deceased and on the pain that we are experiencing in the present moment. With time and work, however, we begin to look towards our future again. You may find yourself making plans – for next week, for next month, for next year. This means that your investment in your own life and living are returning, and this is a good thing.

- **Forgiveness** – We are very careful when we talk about forgiveness. Some people do not feel that anyone needs to be forgiven – that their loved one was ill and died from this illness (e.g., depression). Therefore, it was not something that needs to be forgiven. On the other hand, sometimes people feel that the suicide was an unforgivable choice – one that has hurt other people and should never be "excused." Likewise, some survivors have trouble forgiving themselves for "failing" their loved one. They may believe that they can never be forgiven for their inability to protect their loved one or to prevent the suicide.

  So what does it mean to "forgive"? First, we believe that forgiveness does *not* mean forgetting what has happened. Nor, if you believe an injustice has occurred (for example, that a mental health professional failed to do their job in preventing the suicide), does it mean that you need to somehow accept that injustice? *Rather, we believe that forgiveness means making a choice – often a very difficult choice – to no longer hold on to the anger about what has happened.*

  While it is not our role to tell you to forgive, we can tell you about our experiences with survivors around this issue. In coping with the suicide of a loved one, many people have told us that deciding not to let the anger dominate their life was an important step that helped them tremendously on their grief journey. Survivors have told us that, for them, forgiveness was a way of saying "In spite of what has happened, I want to feel happiness and peace again in my life." They pointed out that forgiveness is also is a way of acknowledging the fact that we do not control the universe and cannot prevent all bad things from happening. Survivors have reminded us that it can be very, very difficult to forgive a person they felt had some role in the suicide of their loved one—a family member, in-law, friend of the deceased, a mental health professional, or even the person who took their own life. At this point in your life you may have chosen not to forgive and that is your right. But again, those who tell us they did find a way to forgive eventually found that they were no longer a prisoner of their own anger. *People forgive, not only to help someone else, but also to help themselves.* To put it differently, forgiveness means moving from anger or guilt towards something more like acknowledgment and regret.

This applies equally well to your anger with yourself. You are not perfect, and you make mistakes. Those mistakes can include how you interacted with your loved one over the course of your relationship and how you responded to their suicidal behavior. Forgiveness means accepting your mistakes and deciding not to continue to be angry with yourself. It means acknowledging that you cannot undo what has happened - and that being angry with yourself will only create more suffering in the world without doing any good. If you have not yet forgiven yourself or someone else, our question to you is, "What would it take for you to begin to do so?"

- **Peace/Acceptance of what happened** – This is the place to which we hope you will be able to arrive. It is a state of mind of non-judgmental acceptance of what has happened, forgiveness for yourself and others, and internal peace with yourself. Not an easy place to reach, is it? Perhaps no survivor ever fully gets there. But we know that, over time, survivors are capable of coming to terms with what has happened and are able to move on with their lives – changed people, but changed in some good ways as well as bad, and able to recommit to life. Based upon the many stories of survivors' journeys we have witnessed, we have written this book in the genuine hope that you, too, will be able reach this state of equanimity.

Conclusion

Human beings have a remarkable capacity to recover from catastrophe. Just look at how individuals, families, even whole communities and nations, have rebuilt themselves after living through terrible events such as war, natural disasters, and plagues. The long journey of coping with loss is never, ever easy. It is a slow, sometimes arduous process. *But if you look around at the world, you can see that it does happen. People do heal - and slowly rebuild their lives while keeping the memory of their loved one in their mind and in their heart.*

In our work over the years we have been on many journeys with survivors of a suicide loss. Again and again we have been witness to the amazing ability of human beings to cope with and even grow from the terrible tragedy of suicide. In the next section, Stories of Survivors, you will see evidence of this change. We include them because our overriding goal for this book has been to offer information and inspiration to people like you, who are grieving a suicide loss. Please hold on to your hope for the future when the pain will ease and wisdom will grow. Realize that a survivor is just that: someone who has managed to survive and grow stronger after the suicide of a loved one. We wish you our best as you travel this difficult journey. Travel safely, with courage, and with hope.

SURVIVOR NARRATIVES:
Stories of Hope and Healing

Vanessa McGann

I lost my oldest sibling, Nadine McGann, to suicide almost 10 years ago. She was 43 years old – younger than the age that I am now. She had never attempted suicide before, though she had spoken about it for years. Many survivors wonder "why?" but for me the reasons were both numerous and obvious. She had run out of an inheritance that had been keeping her afloat; she saw my brother and I start families and felt she would always be alone; ECT and psychiatric drugs (that help so many) had all but destroyed her ability to think, remember or react– a terrible blow because she had always been the smart one, the intellect and scholar. She had also stopped taking the one medication that seemed to incrementally help because she felt that it made her too fat. There were smaller but no less real reasons I could list, all contributing to her feeling that she was a burden, or overlooked, or not capable, or not special. I suppose I should add that she had unremitting treatment resistant unipolar depression, but for me, that reason falls short. I know many survivors feel comfort in seeing suicide as the simple result of a medical/mental illness and I don't take this away from them - but in thinking about Nadine, I feel there was an overreliance on seeking the next drug cocktail or brain stimulator for her cure. It too often reduced her soul to symptoms and pointed her hopes toward an amelioration of side effects rather than an expansion of her dreams.

I tell people that, though in many ways Nadine's suicide was not a surprise, it was a total shock. In fact, Nadine's psychiatrist called me the night she died, worrying about her; we both spoke to her and did our best assessments (I am a psychologist), and we both decided a hospital was not the answer – she was not "at imminent risk" or so they say. I do not and never did blame us for this (only in retrospect poor) judgment call; in her case, she was determined, or perhaps she was in more of a "living zone" at the time we spoke than she was just a few hours later. I feel it is important to tell this part of her story because for many, they blame themselves or their loved one's therapist for missing signs. And though I feel we can do better at preventing suicides in general, I think in the moment, we all do our best.

I suppose I got through the first few hours and weeks "as well as could be expected." Most of what I went through was inchoate grief. But I did have one main concern - my kids. I was so angry with my sister for leaving me this legacy of suicide. I didn't know how broken I was going to be and I didn't want my brokenness to impact my children. I also didn't know how her suicide would directly affect them – I feared for their adolescences and for their knowledge of what solution she had chosen to end her pain. I also want to add that I remember feeling some relief – for me, because I no longer had to worry about Nadine – and for her, because she was done with her pain.

In the very beginning, I was numb and shocked and I was feeling – both physically and emotionally – things I had never felt before. The intensity made me scared that I might lose my mind; I feared that the experience might literally break me. And I could not understand why there were not more resources for me. Especially as a psychologist, I could not understand why this grief was not more widely explored, discussed, or understood.

The first six months were quite awful. Some friends were supportive but most were not – or they were initially and then vanished. Grieving was exhausting and I still had to function for my family and work. In many ways, work was a respite. As a psychologist, my patients did not know of her death. For some reason, this gave me a bit of space to function "as I was before." Yet despite my love of the work, I became disenfranchised from my field. Oddly, I found my mental health colleagues, supervisors, and friends to be the least supportive - if not outright harmful - to me. It became almost unbearable to feel all of these secondary losses. At a certain point, I was so discouraged with the mental health field that I thought I would quit. Almost at that moment, I happened upon an article written by a psychologist in California who had lost her brother to suicide. We spoke at length of shared experiences and she invited me to a conference of the American Association of Suicidology. It was there I met a truly supportive community and began to see that it was not my grief that was "driving me crazy." Instead it was the stigma and lack of support and understanding which this type of loss is associated with that made things so hard for me. From that point, I started to heal.

I have since become an advocate for clinicians who have lost a patient or family member to suicide. I teach, write and train on the subject, and I see bereaved clinicians in my practice. I also work with others bereaved by suicide. Though I don't think one has to be a "suicide survivor" to be a good clinician to this group, I think that my understanding of the stigma, the confusion, and the pain do help. I have heard many stories of therapy that felt judgmental or harmful to those bereaved by suicide and so I also teach and train about unique aspects of clinical work with survivors. In addition, I work with families and children to help them explain, make sense of, and grow from these losses. All of these things have helped me with my grief. It is an honor to share in someone's pain and in their process of putting pieces back together.

In the beginning there was no gift, no silver lining. There was fear of the future and there was pain from the past. But I can honestly say that I now reach moments of deep connection – with my children, my family, my patients and my friends, that I was too anxious or distracted or hurried to experience before Nadine's death. I know I am also a better therapist. I feel I have the ability to look at aspects of struggle and particularly of death – the grief, the longing, the fear – and not turn away. In addition, I have gained a community and a group of friends which are stronger and more reliable than the ones I had a decade ago. What is perhaps most rewarding is being with my kids and being comfortable with the fact of Nadine's suicide. They know how she died but they also know about how she lived. That she was a feminist, she loved dogs, loved reading, loved 50's kitsch. Although they have yet to hit adolescence and go through life challenges, I believe my way of handling the fact of her death, while loving them and teaching them throughout the process, has made them stronger and more loving individuals.

Franklin Cook

My father, Joseph Hickman Cook, was among the millions of men in the 1940s and '50s who, after a stint in the military, went about their business getting a stable job, raising a family, and living in concert with the suburban values of owning a home, being a good neighbor, and following the rules.

That all ended for him in 1978 when, at the age of 49, he died by suicide. At the time, he was in the process of retiring medically from a career with the federal government. His health problem was not severe, but the transition to retirement triggered in him a major depressive episode intensified by paranoid delusions that generated "evidence" about how the government "knew" he had committed a crime. If one takes the short view, he died because the depression that befell him was acute, horrible, and debilitating to the point where he actually lost his mind; and if one takes the long view, he died because he was a lifelong albeit high functioning alcoholic who didn't effectively attend to his emotional health. Whatever view one takes, he did not ever—during the entire course of his life—get the help he needed for the problems that killed him, and that's a pity.

Before my father died, my mother, my three brothers, and I (who were young adults by then) had not a clue among us about the intricacies of mental illness. We were entirely bowled over by the severity and stubbornness of his condition. So—as our father and husband was being "pursued" by the FBI and refusing to come to the phone because it was "tapped"—we got the best medical advice we could, which wasn't much good at all. We tried to give him all of the love and understanding we could, which was to no avail. His depression continuously and then precipitously worsened; four months after the depression began, he was admitted to a psychiatric hospital; two days after being admitted, he mortally wounded himself; and after 24 hours lying in a coma in intensive care, he was dead.

I cannot say much about coping with grief the first 12 years after that, so I'll fast forward: In 1990, I got clean after being an addict since my teenage years. I was 36 and living in my mother's basement; had been divorced twice and estranged from my children; got by from paycheck to paycheck; and was pretty much just glad to be alive. Like my father, I was a highly functioning addict, so I had also accomplished a lot in those years, earning a master's degree, starting a career, eventually repairing relations with my children, and almost always having a job and being able to "look good" on the outside.

I spent the early '90s working on my "issues," and most prominent among them was that I felt as angry with my father and as guilty about his suicide as I ever had. I did everything I possibly could to discover the "key" to all that haunted and tortured me about his act of self-destruction, and many things did help me. My family's and friends' love helped, as did counseling, compassion for my father, meditating, learning about suicide and mental illness, helping others, taking long walks, sitting with my pain instead of running from it, and not giving up—but no single thing by itself was more than a piece of the puzzle. All of it was necessary, and the only explanation I have for being where I am today is that I traversed enough ground to get here, step by step. I grieved by trial-and-error, and my healing turned out to be a holistic experience that I couldn't have caused using a linear strategy. Even at this moment, the path is unfolding as I travel it.

I could have written all of the above 15 years ago to describe my transformation from a person who wasn't surviving to a person who was—but that is only part of the story. My life has been transformed yet again since then, a process that began during a very dark and painful time for me. In the summer of 1999, I was suffering from a major depressive episode of my own. During an eight-month period, I lost 25 pounds, woke up nightly in the wee hours steeped in anxiety, and could not shake almost constant suicidal thinking (though I did not want to kill myself). I was unspeakably frightened because my suicidal thoughts felt beyond my control, and I worried that I might lose my mind as my father had. Fortunately, I got treatment for my depression and joined a peer-led suicide grief support group, which took my recovery and healing to another level—and even led me to a new career.

I began working as a volunteer in community-based suicide prevention and grief support in late 1999, and since shortly after that, I have been a full-time professional in the field. My work today has me helping the newly bereaved, advancing the cause of men's suicide prevention, and collaborating with others who are taking action to save lives and to help people cope with the pain and suffering that leads to suicide or follows it. I share meaningful time with hundreds of survivors, and although I will always be saddened by the reason we are all in this together, I do not think in terms of what should or shouldn't have been. My father is dead, he died horrifically, and his death nearly shattered his loved ones in its wake—and I cannot change that. Even so, his death helped me know that I could change my own life, and compelled me to do so. I was blessed to be able to see the need for deep change in my life, and I am blessed every day to have a chance to keep finding my way from here to there. My father lives on for me in the reality of those blessings.

© 2014 Franklin James Cook. Reprinted by permission. First published by Grief after Suicide at bit.ly/suicidegriefblog.

Bill & Beverly Feigelman

We lost our 31 year-old son Jesse to suicide eleven years ago. Outwardly, Jesse may have appeared to be a least likely candidate for suicide. Handsome, charming, and talented, Jesse had many good things going on in his life in the months preceding his death. He was a film-maker, and just three years previously, had raised half a million dollars to make his debut feature film that was well received in the film industry. Just six weeks before the death he became engaged to the love of his life and he had a great many friends.

Yet, we recognized that beneath his usually upbeat exterior there was a deeply troubled young man. Eight years previously, while staying at our summer home to complete his senior year film project, he lost two of his closest friends to a boating accident after they took a whimsical rowboat ride on an early January day in Northern waters. Jesse harbored great and lasting guilt over their deaths. Despite his eventual ability to transcend this tragedy and make his debut feature film by age 28, his film-making career seemed to have stalled. He thought his feature film would usher in a stream of steady new film work, but it hadn't and instead he was receiving a near constant flood of bills from earlier film making expenses, while he worked temporarily as a clothing salesman in a fancy men's clothing store catering to those in the entertainment industry, a job he felt humiliated him. He felt great pressure from his fiancée, who had high reaching achievement aspirations. His personality was ill suited for a career in the arts with highly self-critical predispositions. Ultimately, his near life-long fascination with self-medication and drug-taking and his mixing of recreational and prescribed drugs led him to impulsively take his life by hanging.

Like most parents bereaved by suicide, we felt the usual mixture of grief, shock, sadness, guilt, confusion, shame, anger and isolation as our lives were turned upside down by the loss of our first born. We both felt greatly helped by the support group we joined almost immediately after Jesse's death. Friends' and family's support and compassion were perceived as essential to us during those early difficult days. We both went to a grief counselor but I was quickly turned off upon detecting the counselor's lack of familiarity with suicide. Bev continued with individual bereavement counseling but experienced rejection and stigma when she was initially invited by her counselor to join a mothers' support group. One of the other bereaved mothers attempted to invalidate Bev's grief by saying, "unlike my son, your son wanted to die." We both read voraciously all the available literature on suicide bereavement. We both found unexpected responses of support for our grief from some family and friends, and disappointing responses of avoidance and unsupportive silences from others.

As I, a professional sociologist, became acutely aware of the limitations of the suicide bereavement literature, I resolved to complete a major study of this subject and began to attend the professional conferences, to establish contacts with other researchers in this field and with the wider community of suicide bereaved people. As I refocused my academic and professional goals, Bev joined me in these and related endeavors; and we both undertook training to become support group facilitators. We became advocates for social change to de-stigmatize suicide and improve mental health treatment availability, and we engaged in fund-raising projects for suicide prevention and research. In addition, Bev, an MSW clinical social worker, joined the clinician-survivors- listserve of the American Association of Suicidology for additional support. About six years after our son's death, we decided to establish our own survivors' support group, to serve suicide-bereaved families in a highly populous, less well served area of our community. As new research findings emerged from our co-authored book, written with two leading bereavement psychologists, about parents bereaved by suicide and drugs, entitled ***Devastating Losses***, we began to address grief professionals, health care practitioners and the bereaved alike with presentations of our findings, throughout the US and in other countries. All these activities seemed to be positive things to do to help sustain the memory of our departed son and to channel these memories into socially helpful directions.

We feel that the cornerstone to our own adaptation–and one for all suicide bereaved others--is that the survivor must establish a 'new normal' for him or herself. The survivor must recognize that many previous life goals are no longer attainable. They must re-set their goals to ones that make sense, and are perceived to be within their potential grasp. They must also engage in sense-making about the death, understand as best as possible why their loved one died and then accept that definition of the situation. Trying to make the world a better place, especially for the suicide-bereaved, has been at the forefront of our new goals. While other survivors may set other new goals for themselves, it is desirable if survivors can think of new goals that will honor their lost loved one's memory by what they do, and do things their lost loved one would have been proud of, if they were still living. That's about the best that can be done in their absence.

Rob Desmond

My brother Jerome was the third of six children. Our family consisted of three boys and three girls. We were a big family but not all that uncommon in the 70s. Jerome was perhaps known as the wild one of the group for the mischievous things adolescent boys do. I'd say he was simply the creative one. He did things because he was bored – and unlucky because he always seemed to get caught.

This carried through high school where he wasn't the recipient of the best grades but always scored well on any tests. He enlisted in the Navy a few years out of high school. I don't think it was his idea as much as it was my father's. Nonetheless, he enrolled and it was the beginning of a downward spiral for him. The relentless order/structure wasn't good. Being told to do mundane tasks for what appeared to be no clear reason other than to stay busy was maddening for him. Perhaps it was the catalyst for his suicide, I am not sure, but his first attempt to take his life was here. His second was here too and led to him receiving an honorable discharge.

In the beginning after my brother's death, I didn't cope, I ran. I went back to work after a week, put my head down and worked…. and worked, and worked. After all, being a male, it was the "right thing to do." What wasn't obvious to my co-workers during the day was that I would go home every night and cry myself to sleep.

I am fortunate to have a large family and a great group of friends. You would think it would be comforting to have such a team around to help me get through a time I'm not sure I can accurately describe in words. My family and I can lean on each other, right? Well, for me, I couldn't find comfort anywhere. Not with my siblings, parents, girlfriend, friends, books, work - nowhere.

Everyone tried. My friends would take me out, my girlfriend would try and schedule things for us to do, my family tried to get together more often, but none of this worked. To me, it all seemed synthetic or manufactured. No one was addressing the elephant in the room and it was maddening to me – though I wouldn't talk about it either.

After almost a year of riding a pent up emotional roller coaster, being asked if I was ever going to be 'normal' again, or why I was so angry all of the time, I knew I needed a change. I didn't know what that change was supposed to be but I knew I needed something. So

I asked for a transfer, and I picked up and moved a few states away where I didn't really know anyone.

On the surface, I was excited because as they say, change can be healthy. What I didn't realize at the time was now that I was far enough away from my friends and family, I was all alone to face my brother's death. Looking back, this was the most important step in my journey of learning to understand why someone so loved, so funny, and so smart would want to leave.

After a month of crying myself to sleep and being outside my support/activity circle of friends or family, under the advice of my sister, I went to a Survivors support group meeting. My life changed.

Being a male and not growing up in a home where we were encouraged to openly express our feelings, I had the wrong definition of a support group. I thought this was a place where people complained to one another or went to get free advice. What I realized after that first meeting was that I couldn't have been more wrong.

The meeting was held in a local school, and not being from the area, I got lost and walked in late. This was a bit of divine intervention as the only seat available in the circle of twenty desks was the one immediately to the left of the person talking. Meaning, if I were to talk, I would go last. Phew.

I sat and listened. I listened to a father talk of the loss of his son, a mother of the loss of her mother, and friends talk about the loss of friends. "FINALLY, there are people who can relate to how I feel!" I remember thinking as the stories went around the group. Then, the one story that I will remember for rest of my life came from a 14 year-old boy who talked with such courage and strength about his father. His father was a police officer and had used his service revolver to take his life. This young man talked about having to see his father, check to see if he was alive, call 911 and then call his mother to tell her the news.

Attending this meeting was the single most influential factor in my learning to cope with my brother's death. This was the catalyst for me to learn more about why he died, the struggles he faced, and the life he ultimately didn't want to live. Thank you young man. I'm sorry to have met you where I did, but I am a better person for having met you.

What you may find interesting is this was the first and only support group meeting I attended for the next 12 years. I realized I was not alone and the feelings I had – the sorrow, the anger, the unexplainable grief – weren't unique to me. There were, unfortunately, many other people who could relate.

For me, and this wasn't an immediate realization based on my own stigma around suicide, I came to understand that what my brother did was not self-centered. When he decided to take his life, his intentions were not to make life difficult for my family or me. It's just the opposite. He didn't want to burden those he loved most with his problems.

I've also come to learn that suicide is a difficult topic for many. I've learned not to judge others who may frustrate you – and they will – by what they say or do. They simply don't understand. I don't hide how my brother died and if it makes someone uncomfortable, I tell them they shouldn't be because I'm not. I'm not ashamed of how he died. It's sad and I miss him terribly, but I'm honored to call him my brother.

I've also come to realize there wasn't anything I could have done to change the outcome of his life. I fretted over this for a long, long time. Could I have said this, could we have tried that? My brother fought battles of the mind and of the heart -ones that I didn't fully understand at the time but have since grown to admire him for fighting so hard. In the end, he had no fight left in him.

Although it has taken me some time, and while I will never fully understand or be able to answer "why?" I am at ease with my brother's decision. It is better for me because I know what he did wasn't cowardly, selfish or the 'easy way out.' I am honored to be called his little brother. Though it was quite difficult for me at first to talk about Jerome's death, I have come to realize I am not honoring his life by hiding how he died. He continues to be a positive influence in my life and if I can help someone else cope with their loss, then we've honored him that much more.

Anita Pandolfe-Ruchman

As I write this is it is hard to believe it has been almost 4 years since my 19 year-old daughter took her own life by hanging herself in her college dorm room. Her death by suicide completely and utterly devastated me, blindsided me and almost destroyed me. But it did not. And miraculously I am alive to share with you now a bit about my journey.

Nora was my youngest child, reared solely by me from the time my marriage ended when she was three years old. We were extremely close and connected. There was never any doubt about how much we loved each other and how much we enjoyed being together. But she was quiet and sensitive and now as I look back, I see how she didn't open up much to share how she was feeling about things. Nora was very bright and inquisitive; she read voraciously and had a smile that melted your heart. She was graceful and kind, always ready to be there for her friends.

Nora's sudden death was utterly shocking and stunning as there was no history of or apparent depression or talk of not wanting to live. She was involved in her new college life, adjusting to her new school and campus. No one knew the pain and hurt she hid inside.

When word reached me of her death I was almost immediately surrounded by friends, and a loving supportive community. Everyone was stunned. I felt so deeply for her friends and boyfriend who were beside themselves with grief and despair.

When I wasn't numb, the pain was searing.

When Nora died I was in the midst of a deep study and exploration of Tibetan Buddhism. Through meditation and retreat I had been exploring the depths of my mind, the nature of reality and the meaning of my life. Not light topics, mind you. These experiences contributed significantly to my ability to survive the nearly mortal wound I suffered due to Nora's suicide.

I decided quite early on to *let people help me*, with food, companionship, shopping, cleaning, etc. I felt like a zombie. I could only get out of bed if someone brought me tea, and then sat on the couch in utter shock and disbelief.

Surprising things helped, such as: Reading the cards and letters every afternoon with my daughter, Lili, and crying together. We made it our daily ritual to make sure we each had some food and a little caffeine, and then take our afternoon 'ride.' It was spring, so we sought out the quiet places by the ocean, driving slowly by while listening to the sound of the surf and the birds. Nora's death catapulted me in to a state unlike I had ever known --- a place beyond words.

Being a nurse, myself, and always helping others with their healing, I knew it would take some radical self-care, time and attention to the unbearable pain if I ever was to heal myself and be 'useful' to anyone else again. There was no way I could return to my job as educator for the psychiatric staff at a large medical Center. I knew I needed to be with this pain to get through it and amazingly I realized that somehow I *would* get through this. So, my world, my life as I had known it, came to a halt. I meditated and prayed for help, I asked for the guidance of my Teachers and therapist. I rested and let go of expectations of *how* and *what* I should be doing. One of my best friends was a bereavement counselor, she showed me lots of useful information about grief and I began to read all I could handle about grief and suicide loss. My daughter, Lili, came to my side and stayed with me for 6 weeks, we mourned together, yet differently as she made a remarkable book on Shutterfly, as a magnificent tribute to her sister. I was immobilized, drinking in the love and connection from my closest friends. We talked about how now we would be looked on as "those poor people whose daughter/sister killed herself." But we also knew we needed to be able to laugh, even though we thought we never *would* laugh again. So every night my daughter would lie next to me and read aloud from the satirical writer, David Sedaris. Miraculously we heard ourselves laughing. This small act was like a balm for our wound.

I read about the anger that people feel after their loved one's suicide. I was too sad for me *and* for Nora to *be* angry. I felt that I had missed so much, how could I not know she was suffering so?

I felt deeply that I needed to love her NOW, to honor her, to try to find her again in a new way.

In the early part of the grieving I definitely felt a kind of 'searching,' as if I was constantly doing a scan to try and find her. Where could she be? I kept the large beautiful pictures of her we had from her memorial service all around the house so that I could see her beautiful countenance. This helped me somehow, to see her face. I spoke with and saw her friends as much as I could for it felt like being with them was the closest thing to being with her.

One day, during my first winter after Nora's death, as I sat on the couch alone in my living room, I realized that no one was going to come and heal me, take care of me. I would have to heal myself. The good news was that I happen to be a healer. I would now have to apply what I knew and how I cared for others, to me. I would heal myself; I would take care of myself. One vital way of doing that was to focus on the Spiritual Teachings and the other one was to serve and care for others.

Among the things that have helped:

On-going study and practice of meditation, yoga, and retreat.

Massage Therapy

Psychotherapy with a therapist skilled in post-traumatic loss.

Consulting with a psychologist who specializes in loss due to suicide.

Writing in a journal to Nora.

Taking part in a loss- due- to-suicide support group led by a professional.

Learning about suicide loss through AFSP, taking part in their annual Survivors Day.

Training to help other survivors.

Attending the Compassionate Friends National Conference

Sound Healing and music therapy

Tree Planting and Gardening.

Creating the yearly project I call "Books in Nora's Name"
Donating children's books in her memory.

Memorial Scholarship

Practice of Doing for others, including volunteering for the
hungry and homeless.

Joanne Harpel

Until he suddenly developed bipolar disorder at 26, my brother Steve had enjoyed a huge amount of success in his short life. He was the valedictorian of his high school class and an honors graduate of Yale, where he wrote an award-winning history thesis, sang in an a cappella group (and was renowned for the dry wit of his song introductions), had a column in the Yale Daily News, and fell in love. He went on to get a graduate degree from Cambridge University and then to Harvard Law School. After graduation he married his college sweetheart (and was so popular that he had 11 groomsmen at his wedding) and they spent six months living in Europe before returning to San Francisco, where he'd accepted a position as an attorney at a prestigious law firm. But just before he came back to the States he became manic and suffered a psychotic break. The manic state lasted for about a week after which he fell into a severe depression. We tried to figure out what to do. He saw several psychiatrists on both coasts and was hospitalized more than once. But his case was complicated and we ran out of time. He took his own life less than a year after being diagnosed, and those same young men who'd stood up for him at his wedding were now pallbearers at his funeral.

After Steve's death, I read everything I could get my hands on. This was back before the age of the internet, so I went to Barnes & Noble, found the death shelf, and bought every single book that had the word "suicide" in the title. I wanted to understand about bipolar disorder, about suicide, about dealing with death. And I wanted to read about other people who'd coped with this, learn how they'd coped, and draw strength from their experience. Since I didn't know another soul on this earth who had lost someone to suicide, I felt a strong urge to meet and connect with other people who really understood what I was going through. I went to a suicide survivor conference about six weeks after Steve died and started attending support group meetings the next month. Although I'm not usually much of a group person, I found comfort in the routine (I went at least monthly for about two years) and in being with people who could relate to this alien world I suddenly found myself in. I also went to other support group meetings for people who'd lost siblings, regardless of the cause of death, because the fact that I'd lost my brother was just as big an issue for me as the cause of his death.

I was also fortunate to have a relationship with a wonderful therapist; although she wasn't a grief therapist per se, she helped give me a great deal of perspective on the loss, as well as permission to grieve in my own way. My family situation is complicated and it was sometimes tricky to figure out how to deal with things in the way that was most healing for me.

As I more fully integrated my emotional loss, I became increasingly active in the field, initially by volunteering and eventually by deciding to devote my professional energy to working in the area. I had been a corporate lawyer before, and although I was a good lawyer, I was never going to be a great one, because I had skill, but no passion. Because I had been personally touched by suicide, it was a cause I cared passionately about, and over time I ended up turning it into a full-time career. I realize that my path is not necessarily a typical one, but for me it has been a way to create something meaningful and gratifying out of a tragedy. It has also been a way to keep Steve part of my present – he's not just part of my past, he's someone who's relevant to my life today, as well. I get to talk about him. And say his name. That matters to me.

Perhaps the most difficult lesson for me was that even loving, well-meaning people can't always be there for one another, especially when they're all grieving at the same time. Suicide is a topic that makes many people nervous and uncomfortable, so people say insensitive things – or may say nothing. When you're feeling vulnerable it can be hard not to take that personally. The most important lesson I've learned is to seek out many different types of support and comfort, so that you have lots of resources and people to draw strength from. Taken together, over time, plus your own inner resilience, the healing does come. And don't be afraid to cry. Tears are a tribute.

Kim Ruocco

John and I met in college and fell in love. After college John joined the Marine Corp and soon after we got married. Life in the Marine Corp was exciting, difficult and rewarding. There was a very strong cultural expectation of strength, independence and resilience. This expectation was extended from the Marine to his or her family.

Exposure to trauma, loss and injury is a regular occurrence in military life. It happens all the time in training exercises as well as on combat or non-combat tours. John's first traumatic loss happened when several of his peers died in a helicopter training accident. Following this incident John had symptoms of post-traumatic stress and paralyzing depression. He didn't want to tell anyone for fear of losing his wings, so he literally willed himself out of the depression. He ate well, tried to exercise, prayed and talked to his close-knit support system. When the depression finally lifted he said to me "what a weak thing to do…I will never do that to you again" - as if his sickness was a weakness in him, something that would not have happened if he were stronger.

The day John died was a "perfect storm" of events. A civilian job had fallen through, recent experiences in Iraq were haunting him and he was living separately from his family while he was training to re-deploy. The dreaded depression had also returned. This time I knew he needed professional help and was willing to sacrifice his career to get him the help he needed. I am a clinical social worker and had been worried about him for a while. The night he died I insisted that he get help and he agreed that he needed it. I knew that asking the Marine Corp for help and admitting that he was sick would be the hardest thing John had ever done. I jumped on a plane and flew across the country to support him. Unfortunately, I was too late. John hanged himself in that hotel room just hours after we talked.

At the scene of his death, my first thought was "what am I going to tell our children?" My sons were eight and ten years old. Their Dad was their hero and their coach. How could I tell these two boys that their Dad made it safely back from a combat zone and then took his own life? I began asking everyone around me what I should tell my children. I was told that suicide was a sin and that my kids were too young to understand suicide. I didn't trust my own instincts so I listened. I told my kids that their Dad died in an accident. I kept my kids from their church and I hushed all of my family and friends.

Two weeks after Johns death I was driving the boys to the eldest one's birthday party. From the back seat my birthday boy said, "Mom, I think I killed Dad". I pulled the car over and climbed in the back seat with my boys. My son then explained that when his Dad was home last they were eating nachos together, and he said he asked his Dad if he could put salt on the nachos. His Dad said "no, because too much salt is not good for your heart". My son then admitted that he salted those nachos when his Dad wasn't looking. My son looked at me and said "Dad must have had a heart attack that caused the accident." At this moment I suddenly awoke from my fog. I could see clearly that the only way to survive this was honesty, trust and love. I sat in the backseat of the car and I told the kids the truth. I told them that their Dad was very sick and that he didn't get the care he needed. I told them that at that terrible moment their Dad was in so much pain that he couldn't think of us, he could only think of ending his pain. I admitted that I made a mistake in not telling the truth from the start. I made a promise that from now on I would tell them the truth. I promised that from that moment on they could ask me anything and I would answer as best I could. I also promised them that I would be there for them, that I was going to take care of myself, and that we were going to get through this together.

Once the shock wore off, the real journey began. I had a strong need to connect with others who had experienced this type of loss. I also felt a burning desire to tell others about my husband's struggles in order to help prevent more military suicides. I worried about my sons. They had not only lost their Dad but they had lost their connection to the military, and that had been such a big part of their life. I began searching for help with these issues and I came up with TAPS (The Tragedy Assistance Program for Survivors). The boys and I attended our first seminar in Washington DC about a year after John's death. The boys were assigned military mentors in the Good Grief Camp and I attended sessions on the adult side. While the weekend was extremely healing for the boys, I felt out of place and slightly ashamed of the way my husband died. The sessions I attended did not meet my needs and I left the weekend feeling more alone than ever. After giving it some thought I called the founder of TAPS, Bonnie Carroll, and let her know how I was feeling. I told her that I thought that losing a loved one to suicide was different. I told her about my struggles with spirituality, sin, telling the children, my guilt and how his death had affected my ability to trust my instincts. She listened and finally said, "build it and they would come." Bonnie knew that there must be others out there.

My real healing came as I built a postvention program for military suicide survivors. In this role I was able to fulfill the key components that I have discovered to be essential to a healthy grief process. The first one is connection. I needed to be with others who had experienced a similar loss. It validated my thoughts and feelings and normalized what I was going through. The second was meaning. As I learned more about the multiple issues that contributed to my husband's death, I started to learn more about my family and myself. I began using this knowledge to build a healthier life. The third thing was purpose. I was able to use my experience to help others. Lastly I found hope. I was hopeful that my boys and I could get through this. I was hopeful that I could find some peace and joy again.

Kristine Kuch

I lost my brother Jack to suicide just a few months before what would have been his 25th birthday. Jack was 13 years younger than me and I felt as if I'd just started getting to know him as an adult and a friend instead of as just my little brother. He was a kind, loving, sensitive person – the kind of kid who would pick wildflowers for our mom when he was supposed to be playing the outfield in a Little League game. Jack was extraordinarily creative, always gravitating towards right-brained activities, like set design for his high school drama club and playing the violin. He was an especially talented artist.

Jack had always been moody, but things took a turn for the worse a year or two into college. He was diagnosed with bipolar disorder and struggled with recurrent depression. Just before his death, he had seemed to be on an upswing, which somehow made it even harder to come to terms with his suicide.

Jack shot himself in my parents' home, in his childhood bedroom. My parents weren't home – my mom had received a cancer diagnosis a few months earlier, and they spent that night at the hospital following her surgery. My aunt discovered Jack's body when she went to check on the house the next day. When my dad called to deliver the news, I remember feeling suddenly afraid that he was calling to tell me that something had gone wrong during my mom's surgery. I was completely unprepared for what he actually had to say. After I finally stopped crying, I remember thinking that there was no way I could possibly survive this. I had never in my life felt so much pain.

The thing that helped me most during those first few months was actually other people. I took some time off from work and started seeing a good therapist. A few of my friends were supportive to a degree I could never have imagined – listening when I needed to talk, providing distractions when I was overwhelmed, and making me laugh when I thought I couldn't. I started keeping a journal. At first, I wrote mainly for catharsis, as a way to ease the pain. As time passed I started writing more deliberately, to record things I didn't want to forget – memories of Jack, details of his memorial service, what the first Christmas without him was like. I created what I call my "Jack box" and began collecting mementos to store in it. I had a memorial to him, including his name, tattooed on my forearm.

How is life different? I have a new appreciation for the fleeting nature of time; the realization that you never really know how much time you have with the ones you love, so it's a good idea to make the best possible use of it. I call my parents and my sisters more often, and we never, ever hang up the phone without saying "I love you." Work seems much less important than it used to. Spending time with friends seems more important. Speaking of friends, and other people more generally, I've found that surviving a suicide provides an opportunity like few others to really learn who people are – it tends to expose sides of them you might otherwise never see.

The main thing I'd like to say to new survivors is that they're stronger than they think they are. They can live through this. There will even come a day when they can smile fondly or laugh when thinking about the person they lost.

Monica Nunes

My only child is Tyler Steven Dixon. He was born 1/22/91 and ended his life on 1/21/11. He will be forever 19 in my heart. He was such a wonderful person who as a young child was very curious about things and independent. Things started changing when he arrived in middle school. However he was depressed and started cutting himself, drinking and experimenting with drugs. He also made his first two suicide attempts at age 15, which he told me about. Immediately, I got him enrolled into a Chemical Dependency program where we went once a week to group meetings and counseling sessions. He continued on with school and did succeed in getting his high school diploma.

About 9:30 A.M. on 1/21/11, I sent Tyler a text to ask what his plans were for his birthday weekend. Since I received no response, I thought he was sleeping in or at work. My mom called at 10:30 A.M. and told me she had found him. Naturally I was devastated. The following several days were a blur while we made plans to bury our only child.

After the services I took six weeks off work. I was seeing a counselor throughout all of this. Then I was introduced to a Mom's Group who met once per month for a potluck dinner and had discussions about dealing with this tragic loss. It was of comfort to be able to talk about Tyler to other moms who have also lost a child, even though the losses were varied, suicide, auto accidents, drowning, accidental overdose, or cancer. It didn't matter; we had the one common denominator of having lost a child.

It's now been three years. I've read self-help books along with going to classes and seminars about ways in dealing with the loss of a child. One day something just clicked with me. Was I going to let the grief, as tragic as it is, control my life and define me or was I going to take this heartache and make Tyler proud of how I am honoring his memory? I chose to make him proud. So now I am looking at things differently. As tragic, sad and sudden it was to have had Tyler's door closed on our world, it has opened up a new door. I have met wonderful people, who have also faced terrible hardships. I'm taking so much better care of myself now by going to the gym to exercise, yoga, massages and regular chiropractic visits. All of these things are helping me regain clarity and focus toward a new direction. I have a network of people who know firsthand what I feel like during certain times of the year, and we all support each other. Please know that while it may feel like the end of the world, eventually it does get a little easier to bear. Just hang on to the ones who are there to support you during your good and bad days.

Peggy Marshall

For most of my life, I knew very little about suicide. No need to know, didn't want to know. That changed eight years ago when my husband, Ed, lost a battle with depression and ended his life. Now, I feel as though I've earned a Master's degree in the study of suicide and grief after suicide loss. For me, acquiring this knowledge was a critical necessity in order to survive.

Ed and I were married for 18 years. He was a kind and gentle man with exceptional intellect, outgoing personality and leadership abilities that served him well in the business world. Ed's sense of humor, quick wit and zest for life endeared him to many, but also masked the undercurrent of sadness that haunted him. I knew it was there, but very few others did. Many of his friends were shocked to learn he died by suicide.

I was absolutely devastated by Ed's death. My heart was broken not just by the loss of my beloved partner in life but also by realizing the depth of pain he must have been experiencing to purchase a gun and see death as the only solution. I found him and the visual of this experience replayed in my mind for quite some time.

In the first weeks and months after Ed's suicide, I experienced a terrifying storm of emotions. I felt as though I was inside the funnel of a tornado of sadness. I felt crushed by feelings of abandonment and loneliness and confusion. Swirling questions of "why" and "what could I have done to prevent it" were relentless and overwhelming. At the same time I was angry because I was doing everything I could to help him battle the depression and his suicide felt like betrayal.

What helped me reach up from this downward wind spiral of despair were faith, family, friends and fellow survivors. My immediate family and close circle of friends had never experienced a suicide loss but they encircled me with hugs of love, shoulders to cry on, listening ears and hope for healing. Even more important, they knew I was wrestling with the question of how God could allow this to happen so they encouraged me to seek answers and grab hold of the promises in the Bible. While I don't believe that God wanted Ed to die by suicide, I came to the conclusion that because God is sovereign, he allowed it to happen. Why? I don't and may never understand why, but I do believe in God's repeated promises to comfort us and walk with us through the valley of the shadow of death. And he has delivered on those promises.

One friend sent me a book on suicide loss written by a woman who lost her husband to suicide. As I read about her experience, I discovered I wasn't alone and my feelings were normal for this kind of grief. In addition to encouraging me to read many other books, this author provided a window into survivors of suicide loss support groups. I later attended an 8-week support group, which gave me an opportunity to interact face-to-face and heart-to-heart with people who experienced suicide loss. Hearing the stories of other survivors and telling my story opened the path to healing. Yes, there were tears, but also laughter. We learned that while everyone heals differently, everyone does have the capacity to heal. And one facilitator, who is also a survivor, provided encouragement that healing is possible.

Several years later, I completed training to become a facilitator for survivors of suicide loss support groups. Next, I volunteered to start a local conference for AFSP's International Survivors of Suicide Loss Day. By reaching out to other survivors and sharing insights, I found that it actually helped me continue to heal. And reaching out to others has brought meaning out of my loss – transforming my pain into hope for others.

Healing has been a long journey with lots of stops and starts, wide variations in speed and unexpected discoveries. Will the pain and grief ever completely go away? Probably not, but it won't be as intense. By embracing the grief and learning how to grow from the experience, I have become stronger and able to build a new life filled with joy and love.

So what insights have I learned on my grief journey that might be helpful for those just starting their journey as suicide loss survivors?

- **Hold on to hope, even when you can't see it**. Your friends, family and other survivors can help you hold on to hope during the difficult times. Hope is always there, even on dark, cloudy days.

- **Connect with and learn from other survivors of suicide loss**. You can do this by reading books by survivors, joining support groups or online chat groups. You will find strength in knowing you are not alone and you can learn valuable insights to help you in your journey.

- **Expect a whirlwind of emotions that are difficult to navigate**. Don't run from them or try to bury them. You can't outrun them. And trying to keep them buried won't work and requires too much energy. Your best bet is to acknowledge and process them. Do it in small doses if you have to, but be persistent. And know these emotions will be just under the surface, making surprise visits for quite some time.

- **Understand that grief may manifest in physical ways**. Consider that your body as well as your heart and mind have experienced trauma. I didn't make this connection at first, so I thought that in addition to losing my mind *(by not being able to concentrate),* my body was also falling apart. Know that it is not unusual for your immune system to be compromised, leaving you more susceptible to illnesses. Emotions of grief can also be expressed in lower back pain or other areas. Remember to take good care of yourself by eating healthy foods, getting enough sleep and exercising regularly. Consult your doctor if problems appear.

- **Realize that your life will never be the same but you can still have heartfelt joy**. It's not realistic to expect our lives to remain the same after the tragic loss of loved ones. How could it be without our loved ones there? A scar will remain along with the treasured memories and love. And as the healing progresses, we discover that the depth of pain we experienced brings with it the capacity to feel joy at a greater depth. We also find that our compassion for others increases.

- **Look for ways to learn from the loss or make meaning.** As you work through the grief, take time to reflect and see if there is something you can learn from the experience. Maybe it has something to do with taking better care of yourself. Maybe it is learning how to connect more deeply with others. Maybe it is learning how to ask for help. Maybe it is learning how to cope with stress and loss. Whatever it is, don't miss the opportunity to learn and enhance your life. And later when the time is right, you may want to find a way to reach out and share your insights with other survivors who are just starting their grief journey. Doing so has been a healing salve for my heart.

Dennis Tackett

I will never forget early morning October 11, 2005. I received a call from the Washington, D.C. police department notifying me that my son Jeff had taken his life. I had never imagined what happens to a father mentally and physically after their child has died from suicide.

Jeff was born on March 6, 1979, and I knew he was special from the day he was born. He learned new things easily and embraced learning and exploring. He was musically inclined and was very interested in mathematical challenges. He loved to travel and went to Germany with his high school German club. He graduated third in his high school class with High Honors and many college level credits. He was very structured in high school and did not get into any trouble. He went to the University of Florida under the Lottery Scholar's program with a full academic scholarship. When Jeff died he was a graduate student at American University pursuing a PhD in Economics.

After Jeff started college, I began to think that he might be gay. I confronted him with this suspicion and he finally admitted that he was. It was very brave of him to tell me as I was a retired U.S. Air Force officer and I believe Jeff was scared that I would excommunicate him from the family if I learned this news. I told him that I loved him no matter what and his sexual orientation was not an issue for me or his stepmother Chris. Sadly, Jeff did not receive many positive reactions from relatives. In fact, some even told him that he was going to go to hell. I felt sorry for Jeff because I knew that he would be hurt by rejection, and I felt bad because I knew he would face other people who would judge him harshly.

After Jeff took his life, my wife Chris and I were at a loss as what to do to help ourselves. It was all a blur. I knew we had to deal with paying his bills and handling his estate. I felt like I needed to not show my emotions – that I needed to be strong for my daughter (Jeff's older sister), my wife and also for my mother. But I don't think that I was able to be any help to them either.

About a month after Jeff's death, to try to understand what was happening to us, my wife and I attended a class on grieving at a local hospital, which met once per week for six weeks. Although this class was for people grieving loss from all causes, we learned that our feelings were normal, and most importantly I learned I wasn't going crazy. We also learned about and signed up to attend a Survivor of Suicide (SOS) Day being presented in November. When we walked in, I was shocked to see so many people in this room - they were also survivors of suicide! Up until that point we felt so alone in our loss. Furthermore, I was amazed to see that most of the others seemed able to function – to carry on a conversation, share with others, and even smile and laugh – all we did was cry through the presentation. This gave us some hope that we might someday be able to talk and laugh and feel like we could once again participate in life.

During the SOS Day presentation we watched a short video about the Out of Darkness Walk hosted by The American Foundation for Suicide Prevention (AFSP). We felt like we needed to do the next walk – a 20 mile overnight walk - to try to raise funds and become involved in the cause of suicide prevention.

We spent the next eight months preparing for the Walk. I think it was good that I had something to focus on. Getting ready helped us as my wife and I trained and talked (and cried) together every day. Since the Walk is a fundraising walk, I had to learn to approach people to request donations for suicide prevention. When speaking with friends and coworkers, I was surprised by the number of people who told me about a family member or friend who had died by suicide. Meeting and talking to people at the Walk who had a similar loss to us and learning what helped them cope really had an impact on us in learning to cope with our loss. The impact of talking to others and the support we received at the Walk was so great that we have walked in The Overnight Walk every year since then.

As a father of a child who has taken his own life, I've been plagued with guilt for not being able to protect my son from this monster. I was supposed to be the leader of my family and I felt like I had failed in this key element. I still often remain conflicted by these feelings, even though I know that I was not in control.

My advice to other fathers who have lost a child to suicide is the following:

- Learn that you are not less of a man or less of a father because you have lost a child to suicide.
- Believe that the best way that you can help your family is to help yourself first.

- Do not feel that you are somehow flawed for not being able to protect your child.

- Seek help in any form that you feel may help you. There are professional organizations, support groups, and individuals who can provide a variety of perspectives on how to start healing.

- Realize that the sooner you take action to start healing yourself, the sooner you will be able to find a sense of purpose in your life.

- Remember that others grieve differently than you do and do not judge the way others grieve.

Even 9 years after the loss of my only son Jeff, I continue to slowly heal by allowing myself to talk, cry, and grieve with others who have endured a similar tragedy. I have become involved with AFSP to try to help prevent suicides and to bond with other survivors of suicide who, like me, are working to find ways to move forward.

I know that life goes on, and I want to try to still enjoy it despite having this huge hole in my heart. The support I receive from family, friends, and even strangers helps me through this difficult and ongoing transition. My journey continues.

Nancy Rappaport M.D. Child psychiatrist and associate professor of psychiatry at Harvard Medical School

On the day that my mother died by suicide in 1963, she was preparing for the return of her six children. I was four years old and the youngest of her brood. My mother had been embroiled in a protracted public custody battle with my father for two years, and was devastated when the judge reversed his custody decision.

I remember riding to kindergarten in my father's big station wagon. We usually passed a cemetery along the way. Soon after my mother died, I would jump up and down in the back seat, point out the car window, and gleefully announce in a singsong voice, "There's where Mama is buried. There's where Mama is buried." Like so many children, I blurted out, without inhibition, the unspeakable in my family. If I could have asked, I'd have wanted to know everything: What was my mother like? Did she look like me? What were her favorite foods? How much did she love us? What did my father love about her? Why did they fight? Why was she so unhappy that she would kill herself? Didn't she want someone to save her, and when no one did, was she afraid when she died?

In seventh grade, my blended family of eleven children was heading toward yet another divorce, and I decided to run away to my school. I lasted one night in the school auditorium before I was discovered by my parents and the principal. This precipitated a referral to a therapist, and I made the trek to see Dr. Walter for over four years. Gently, Dr. Walter reassured me that nothing I did or thought had caused my mother's suicide.

If we have a continuous bond with those who die by suicide, I had a more complicated relationship with my mother after the birth of my first daughter. I started to write "Letters to Mama," which came from a deep longing to share with my mother this daughter who I adored. I lamented, I raged, I questioned my mother long gone. For over ten years I reworked these letters, did extensive interviews of family members and friends of my parents, and reviewed court documents and archival newspaper articles. As a child psychiatrist, daughter, and mother, I tried to put all of this together into a meaningful narrative to both heal myself and provide a road map to others.

With the publication of my memoir In Her Wake: A Child Psychiatrist Explores the Mystery of Her Mother's Suicide and sharing my journey with many "survivors," I came to appreciate I was not alone and found confidence that in sharing my truth I put my mother to rest and gave others comfort. I have devoted more than twenty years to training psychiatrists about treating suicidal adolescents, and have also taught educators to support students who are struggling in school. I am sometimes asked if I ended up being a psychiatrist because I lost my mother to suicide and this is somehow my effort to save others, but this is oversimplified. All of us need hope in our darkest moment, and experienced clinicians can help us navigate. At the same time, I have a level of humility and understand that we do the best we can to prevent suicide, but ultimately if there is a completed suicide it is usually a blameless tragedy. This wisdom may come from working through the loss of my mother, and my persistence comes from the belief that we are all loved and deserve care as we find our way.

I am often asked practical advice about how to explain suicide to a child. Here are my suggestions for an understandably overwhelming time.

1. Families may cover up the cause of death because they feel protective of children and do not want to cause pain. It is better to be honest. The best protection is to be truthful, provide comfort and reassurance, and create a nurturing environment that makes children feel safe enough to ask questions.

2. It is important both to validate what children are feeling and to take their lead.

3. Tell children that nothing they do or say caused their relative to die by suicide and make the link that many suicides are connected to mental illness.

4. Be prepared to revisit the loss at transitions such as graduations, marriages, and births.

5. There is no right way to grieve, and each family member may have a different pace or way of grieving.

6. Even though a child of a parent who has died by suicide is five times more likely to kill herself than a child who is not exposed to such a loss, it is still extremely rare (12 deaths per 100,000 people versus 8 per 100,000). So far, researchers have demonstrated that children who have lost a parent to suicide are at greater risk of killing themselves if they have a mood disorder, engage in substance abuse, are "impulsively aggressive," or are exposed to intense conflict in the family. It is still unclear how a parent's suicide increases the risk for these children. But losing a parent this way is also not a

prophetic death sentence; it takes a lot of damage to lose the will to live.

7. Children must know suicide is part of their family medical history, know how to recognize mental illness, and be able to share with an adult if they feel suicidal.

8. Although it is a terrible loss to lose a parent to suicide, children can continue to grow with love, support, and the opportunity to find a narrative that allows them to heal.

APPENDIX A

When to Seek Professional Help & How to Find a Therapist

Deciding to Seek Therapy

Some suicide survivors include therapy with a mental health professional as part of their grief work. Others ask "How do I know when to seek outside help? How do I find a competent therapist?" In this Appendix, we will try to address these important questions. We want to begin by reiterating how crucial it is to take care of your physical and mental health in the aftermath of a suicide. If you were severely injured in an automobile crash, you would expect to go through a period of convalescence where you rested, paid extra attention to your body's functioning, and received professional rehabilitation help. It is not so different when one has experienced an emotional "crash." You must pay attention to your feelings and mood, your thinking, and your behavior, monitoring them for warning signs that extra help may be in order. These warning signs can include:

- Increased use of chemical substances to control the emotional pain

- A depressed mood that grows steadily worse over time, particularly if it includes hopelessness and thoughts of ending your own life

- Anxiety symptoms that significantly interfere with functioning, such as difficulty leaving the house or panic attacks

- Excessive avoidance of other people and socially isolating yourself

- Intrusive flashbacks of your loved one's death

- Active avoidance of any reminders of the death

- Difficulty functioning at work or at home that does not gradually improve with time

- On-going disruption and tension in your relationships with other people as a result of the suicide

- Extreme and persistent denial of the reality of the death.

121

All of these symptoms can be common in the beginning of the grieving process. However, if they persist or increase, rather than gradually decreasing over time, they are indications that a consultation with a mental health professional is in order.

For some people, the idea of seeking mental health treatment is mysterious, frightening, or just plain "weird." They may have mistaken ideas about what therapy is about, or how it can be of help. For years, the popular media have portrayed mental health clinicians and the people who seek their services in very stereotyped ways. Therapists may be portrayed as "crazy" themselves, and the people who need treatment as dangerous and out of control. Suicide survivors in particular may be suspicious of mental health clinicians and the mental health system. They may feel that this system failed their loved one and contributed to the eventual suicide.

So, what is therapy really about? Put simply, talk therapy (as opposed to medication) is an on-going dialogue between two people. It is a partnership where one of the individuals has special knowledge and skills at helping the other person tackle their difficulties and improve their life. It must always be based on a relationship where the client trusts and feels understood by their therapist; and the therapist shows respect, compassion, and knowledge of the problems for which the client is seeking assistance. Therapy has some of the characteristics of a close and confiding friendship, except that a friendship involves reciprocal give and take, whereas the therapy relationship is one-directional, with the clinician focusing on the needs of the client (and being paid, as a professional, to do that). While the heart of therapy is this secure relationship and the honest conversation that it engenders, it can also involve the use of specific techniques that are targeted towards particular issues or problems. This includes grief counseling (also called grief therapy).

What Should I Look for in a Therapist?

- **Credentials** – many people assume that all mental health professionals are trained and qualified to deal with loss and grief as a presenting problem. If only that were true! While many therapists list grief counseling as something that they provide, very few therapists actually *specialize* in grief counseling. You may be surprised to find that there is not even any official or agreed upon definition of what constitutes the profession of grief counselor, nor what the standards are for someone to call themselves by that name. There are some organizations that certify people as grief counselors after taking a few online bereavement related courses, but there are only a handful of accredited universities that offer regular degrees in grief counseling or bereavement studies. Moreover, to the best of our knowledge, no state in the United States specifically licenses people as grief counselors.

So what credentials should you look for? First, we recommend that the individual should have a degree in one of the recognized mental health professions, which include: psychiatrist, clinical psychologist, psychiatric nurse or nurse practitioner, licensed clinical social worker, licensed marriage and family therapist, or licensed mental health counselor. *All of these professionals will have a foundation in understanding mental health problems and doing therapy, although they may or may not have much experience in working with bereavement as a presenting problem.*

Second, since there are very few credentialing programs specifically in grief counseling, *you should feel completely free to inquire about the therapist's additional training and experience in dealing with grief, including grief after suicide.* A therapist should be comfortable in telling you how much training they have in dealing with bereavement, including training in graduate school and additional continuing education courses. They should also be able to tell you how often they work with suicide bereavement as a presenting problem. It is also okay to ask whether they are a survivor themselves. We do want to emphasize that it is not absolutely necessary that your therapist be a survivor themselves. But, you should look for at least a minimum of experience and training in doing this work with bereaved clients before you decide to start therapy. After all, if you had a heart attack, you would certainly want to know that your cardiologist had treated many other people with heart disease. Choosing a therapist after a suicide is no less important for your mental health. Please be aware that it is perfectly acceptable and, we believe, even a good idea to "shop" for a therapist until you find one that you feel confident can be of help to you. Begin your search by checking with family and friends who may have seen a therapist, with your primary care physician, or with your local mental health center or hospital based psychiatry department. The state professional associations of psychiatrists, psychologists, marriage and family therapists, and social workers in your area will also likely offer a referral service. And local hospices and grief support groups in your area may have clinicians who do a lot of grief counseling and to whom they regularly refer. Be sure to explain that you would like someone who specializes in working with bereavement when you contact any of these potential referral resources.

- **Personality and Compatibility** – finding a good therapist is a little like finding a good marital partner. It takes a certain amount of searching, mutual effort, and "good chemistry." Even when a therapist is competent and knowledgeable about grief, it does *not* mean that they are the right therapist for *you*. Above all, you should feel emotionally safe with your therapist. After all, you are talking about what may be the greatest psychological injury of your lifetime, and you are probably feeling pretty confused, fragile, and vulnerable. *In order to work well with a therapist, you must have a feeling of trust in their competence to help you, as well as their basic compassion and caring for you.* In addition, as you work with them, you should experience a growing sense of being understood – that even if they have not lived through the same loss as you, they work hard at understanding what your loss means for you. You should also have a growing appreciation of the competence of your therapist – that they "know the landscape" of this kind of loss, and are not frightened of or judgmental about the intensity of your grief. It is also good when a therapist has a certain amount of humility about "knowing what they don't know." By this, we mean that even if a therapist is experienced and skilled, they should recognize that *you* are the real expert on *you*, not them. They should be open to discovering (along with you) what this loss means just for you, and open to your own ideas of what you need and what will be helpful for you in your journey. You should feel that they are authentically interested in you as a unique individual who is experiencing a great loss – not just a diagnostic category or another "bereavement case" in their practice. Lastly, although therapists are trained to keep their own personality in the background, you should have a sense of liking your therapist as a person. Put differently, you should believe that your therapist is a kind, compassionate, and genuinely caring individual with whom you can be authentically open. All of these factors are crucial in choosing the right person with whom to work.

Expectations for Therapy: What Grief Counseling Can and Cannot Do

Sometimes people have a pretty realistic expectation for therapy – and sometimes they do not. In addition, grief counseling is different from most other types of therapy in that a large part of the work involves coming to terms with something that cannot be changed – rather than working on something that can be changed, such as an aspect of one's behavior, thinking, or feelings. Grief counseling can have as its goal the reduction of distress, a restoration of an ability to feel hope and happiness, and the learning of new and more adaptive ways of coping with the loss. But at its heart, grief counseling is about having a skilled professional journeying with you as you come to terms with the loss of your loved one and its impact on your life.

Here are some things that therapy can do for you:

- **Provide information** – You should receive accurate information about the normal range of responses to a suicide, the various coping strategies that a person can take along the path toward getting better, and some of the predictable "hard spots" such as upcoming difficult dates during the year and dealing with difficult people. The territory of grief after a traumatic death is unfamiliar to most people (including some therapists), and a clinician who can help you sort out what is "normal" can be extremely valuable as a guiding reference point for your own progress. A knowledgeable therapist will also be able to direct you to additional helpful resources such as support groups, websites, articles, books, and videos.

- **Reality Testing** – Suicide often leaves the survivors with a flood of agonizing "Why?" and "What if?" questions – why did they do this, what were they thinking, why didn't I see it coming, why didn't I prevent it? These questions are both common, and for many people, a critical area to explore with a non-judgmental but knowledgeable person. A clinician who understands both suicide and the grief of suicide survivors can help you sort out how realistic your "hindsight" is about the death, and the ways that you may be unfairly holding yourself responsible for the death. They can help you better understand the underlying factors that create the "perfect storm" that creates suicide, and gain a more realistic perspective about the complex factors that contributed to your loved one's death.

A word of caution is in order, though. Like many people who are confronted with the intense guilt that survivors can experience, some therapists try to prematurely resolve these difficult issues of guilt too quickly, pointing out that the self-blame is "irrational." In other words, upon hearing statements such as "I should've," "Why didn't I?" "If only...", some therapists respond with, "You shouldn't feel guilty because... ."*In contrast, we have learned that survivors need time and support in working through the feelings of responsibility for themselves, in their own time* – without the therapist pushing the client to get over these feelings. Working this through is one of the central tasks for survivors, and one that cannot be rushed. We often say something like this to new survivors: "I recognize that you will probably need to put yourself *on trial* about this suicide. My goal is that you and I work together to make sure that you have a *fair trial* and that we carefully consider all of the *evidence*. But I understand the need for you to do your own personal investigation of what has happened." This is a therapist who understands what grief (and guilt) after a suicide looks like.

- **Finding Meaning and Perspective** – Suicide is often experienced by the survivor as a senseless act – something that "just doesn't compute." Being able to return over and over again to the story of what happened, why it happened, and what it means in the life of the survivor is also a central task, one that can help with the process of making peace with the death. While no therapist can tell you what the suicide of your loved one means for you, through skillful questioning, compassionate listening, wise observation, and competent but occasional use of some specific techniques, an experienced grief therapist can help you to view the death in a broader and more multifaceted way – one that honors your loved one while acknowledging the great pain that the death has left for the survivors.

- **Dealing with Social Problems** – a very common outcome of suicide is the interpersonal strain and isolation it may create for survivors. This disruption of the bonds within families and with the larger community creates many problems for survivors. A knowledgeable grief counselor can help you sort through these difficulties with other people and offer support as you rebuild or let go of the relationships that have been changed by the suicide.

- **Dealing with Symptoms** – Survivors of suicide loss can suffer from a number of distressing and disruptive symptoms: sleep disorder, lack of energy, panic and post-traumatic "flashback" symptoms, and others. A skilled clinician can recommend behavioral techniques that can help to effectively control and reduce these symptoms for most people, or medication, if needed.

- **Reducing aloneness** – We do not have to tell you: it is inherently isolating to live through an experience that most other people around you have not endured. Sharing all the elements of that experience with a compassionate therapist (as well as participating in support groups and other survivor related activities) can help to reduce the sense of aloneness that has added to your suffering.

Here are some things that therapy cannot do:

- **Turn back time** - Intellectually you know that your loved one is dead and cannot return. But as we discussed in the section on magical thinking, there is still a part of one's mind that miraculously hopes that the death can be undone. Don't be surprised if you feel disappointed that your therapist doesn't have these magical powers to "make everything better" for which you somehow have been looking. They cannot stop all the pain, they cannot answer all of the "why" questions, and they cannot do the one thing that would truly solve your problem – roll back time and stop the suicide from happening. Of course, you know this already – but the wish to somehow wake up and find that it was all just a nightmare is powerful, and so is the wish to find someone who can "fix it all." As therapists, we wish that we could - but sadly, we cannot.

- **Tell you step by step what you need to do** – sometimes people who do not have any experience with therapy expect it to be like a visit to a medical doctor. You present your problem to the therapist, the clinician diagnoses it, and then they tell you what to do to fix it. In other words, some folks expect therapy to be a process of receiving "advice" from an "expert." It is an understandable, if erroneous, belief. In reality, therapy is a mutual problem-solving endeavor, ***with you being the expert on you, and the therapist being the expert at helping you to help yourself.*** Moreover, the grief journey of any two people is never exactly the same - so what is helpful for one person may be less helpful (or even harmful) for another person. As he or she gets to know you better, your therapist can sometimes make very useful and specific suggestions – but mainly, you will find that learning to live in the world after the suicide of a loved one is a trial and error process. It is an expedition where you and your therapist will look for ways of viewing the suicide and coping with the loss that seem true and sustainable for you. Some of them will work, and some won't. But you will have a well-informed and understanding consultant in that process, and that can make a big difference!

- **Answer all of the "Why?" questions** – the truth is, the person who could really answer your "Why?" questions is gone – leaving you with the bewilderment and anguish that unexplainable suicide can cause. One of the tasks for survivors is to learn to live with what one experienced suicide grief counselor calls the "blind spot"– the lack of answers for these aching "Why?" questions. At least to some degree, most survivors have to make their peace with these unanswered questions. And of course, your therapist does not know the answers either. What they can do is assist you in better understanding why suicide happens in general (see Appendix B on *"Understanding Suicide: The Perfect Storm"*), and help you sort out which of these factors might apply in the case of your loved one. But you may never fully understand all the reasons why this happened. The task is to find a way to accept this "blind spot" and go on with your life in spite of the mystery and pain that come with not having answers.

- **Fix problems that existed before the death** – sometimes people who have lost a loved one to suicide also struggle with other problems in their life. These problems might be related to the suicide (e.g. if the breadwinner in the family dies by suicide, then the surviving partner may face significant financial problems), or they may be unrelated. Like anyone else, survivors can wrestle with substance abuse, psychiatric disorders, dysfunctional relationships, health problems, etc. It is common that these additional life problems are worsened by the loss of someone to suicide – and they often need to become an additional focus of therapy - with your current therapist, or if they not equipped to treat these problems, then through referral to a specialist in the disorder (e.g., referral to a substance abuse program for someone with a drinking problem). You and your therapist should pay attention to the ways that these other problems may be affecting your progress in your grief recovery, and decide together the best ways to deal with these issues.

Medication

The use of psychotropic medication (drugs that are designed to influence a person's mood, thinking, or behavior) as an adjunct in bereavement care is a source of controversy among both grief counselors and their clients. Some survivors are quick to refuse the use of any medication, for any reason, when grief is the presenting problem. They may feel that that these medications suppress grief. They might argue instead that grief is a natural response to loss, and drugs create an artificial feeling of wellbeing when it is not normal to be feeling okay. In addition, some people have concerns that medications are increasingly offered as the first line of treatment for problems of complicated grief – a "quick fix" for harried doctors and for patients seeking immediate relief from painful emotions. The case is often made that the use of psychoactive medication is part of a larger societal discomfort with grief - encouraging people to "get over" their grief as quickly as possible so that they can "move on." And still, other folks just have a general dislike of the feeling that "I'm not in control of my own thoughts and behavior if I take a drug like that." In the case of suicide, sometimes survivors may also feel that the inappropriate use of medications contributed to their loved one's death, and they consequently have a general suspicion of any psychoactive medications.

On the other hand, some clinicians argue that the failure to provide immediate treatment for bereavement-related depression (usually anti-depressant medication) is a kind of malpractice. They believe that clinicians have an obligation to use all of the tools at their disposal to help treat these serious problems. They point to the considerable research evidence that modern anti-depressant and anti-anxiety medications—**along with counseling-** can be very helpful in relieving the symptoms of depression or anxiety disorders. And they also note that the reports of some anti-depressant drugs actually contributing to suicidal thoughts or behavior apply to only a very small percentage of people using the drugs (mostly adolescents or young adults).

Our own experience with clients has led us to what we believe is a balanced and sensible "middle ground" stance about the use of these drugs after traumatic loss. This position can be summed up in a question for both clinician and client to consider: ***"Will the medication be used in the service of the griefwork?"*** That is, will the medication help the survivor progress towards healthy management of their grief? If the answer is yes, then medication may be an important part of the overall treatment plan for a bereaved individual. Note that we say "an important *part*." In our opinion, we believe that medication should rarely, if ever, be the sole method of treatment when bereavement is the presenting difficulty. We do not agree with a professional who "treats" a bereaved person by simply writing a prescription and sending the person on their way. And if the answer to the question *"Will the medication be used in the service of the griefwork?"* is "No", then clinician and client alike must ask themselves "Why would I take these drugs, and for whose benefit am I taking them?" Let's elaborate on this position.

Recall that one of the most important tasks for people who are traumatically bereaved is to learn how to "dose" their grief. Dosing means that, at times the person allows the feelings of grief to come – *and,* at other times the person is able to put the grief-related thoughts and feelings aside when other tasks need to be accomplished (such as functioning at work or being with one's children). The right medication given at the right time can be very helpful in treating the symptoms that may be interfering with a person's functioning (e.g., trouble sleeping). ***It is important to understand that medication treats symptoms, not life problems.*** Medication can be very helpful in reducing specific difficulties, such as sleep problems and symptoms of anxiety - but it does *not* solve life problems. And, as you already know, losing a loved one to suicide is a tremendous life problem, not just a symptom. If medication is recommended for you, and you decide to try it, make sure that your prescriber does the following:

- Explains the target symptoms that the drug is meant to treat

- Explains the benefits and risks (including side-effects) of the drugs that you will be taking

- Tells you what you should do if you experience any side-effects or negative outcomes from the drugs

- Follows you regularly (particularly when you are just starting on the drugs) to see how you are doing and to adjust the dosage or type of medication you are taking

- Ultimately, supports you in your right to make the final decision about whether to take the drugs, and if started, when to taper off the medications.

When these guidelines are followed, we believe that the use of medication can be an important tool for helping people who are bereaved by suicide.

APPENDIX B

Understanding Suicide: The Perfect Storm

Over the course of history, suicide has been attributed to many different causes: insanity, moral weakness, cowardice, impulsiveness, character flaws, excess stress, social pressure, social rejection, loss, heroism (as in giving one's life for a noble cause), social disorganization and disruption, the devil - and a host of other explanations. And as we have discussed in this book, most survivors need to create their own personal narrative – an explanation of why their loved one died by suicide. The search to answer the question "Why?" is difficult and probably unique to each suicide. It may also be different for each survivor of a given suicide. So unfortunately, this Appendix cannot tell you definitively why your loved one did what they did. What we can do is tell you some of the general factors that contribute to most suicides, and hopefully this will help you in your own quest to answer the more personal question "Why did *my* loved one end their life?"

Suicide Epidemiology in the USA

It helps to know something about the breadth and depth of suicide within the United States. Suicide is the 10th leading cause of death in America, with an average of nearly 40,000 people dying from this cause of death every year. The rate of suicide in the U.S. has held more or less steady for many years at between 11 and 12.5 suicides per 100,000 people per year - although there have been increases over the past few years. This overall rate, however, masks tremendous differences in the suicide rates for different sub-groups of people. For example, males are almost four times more likely to *complete* suicide than females, although females are about three times more likely to *attempt* suicide than males. Likewise, the suicide rate for the elderly is usually the highest of any age group, particularly for elderly males. Rates are also higher for Caucasians and Native Americans, and lower for African-Americans, with Asian-Americans and Hispanics being in the middle. Although there is less reliable data about suicide attempts (since many people who make a suicide attempt never seek medical or mental health treatment after the attempt), estimates are that there are 20 to 25 suicide attempts for every completion. Survey data show that in a given year, approximately 8 million Americans will have serious thoughts of suicide, 2.5 million will make a plan to end their life, and 1.1 million will have made some kind of suicide attempt. Among youth, suicide is the third leading cause of death, and as many as 16% of students in grades 9-12 report having seriously considered suicide and 7.8% report having made an attempt one or more times in the last year. There are more than twice as many suicides as there are homicides in the U.S., and more people die of suicide than of motor vehicle crashes. A person dies of suicide in the United States approximately every 15 – 16 minutes. *If these facts and figures are staggering to you – and they should be - you are not alone in your surprise.* Suicide remains a tremendously stigmatized, under-reported, and poorly understood cause of death - yet these numbers make clear that it is a *major public health problem* in America. For more information about the epidemiology of suicide in the United States, please see the websites of the American Foundation for Suicide Prevention (www.afsp.org) and the American Association of Suicidology (www.suicidology.org).

What Causes Suicide?

Suicide is not just a random happening in the universe, nor is it the result of just one simple factor. Instead, like the set of meteorological conditions that are necessary for a tornado or hurricane to develop, suicide seems to require a set of conditions for it to happen. *In other words,* s*uicide is the "perfect storm" – a complex combination of biological, psychological, social, and situational factors that combine in just the wrong way to create the conditions that allow suicide to happen*. What are some of these factors?

- *Psychiatric Disorder. As we stated earlier in the main text, one of the most important contributors to suicide is the presence of a psychiatric disorder, most often the mood disorders of depression or bipolar disorder.* Other psychiatric disorders, such as schizophrenia, post-traumatic stress disorder, substance abuse, and eating disorders also have elevated rates of suicide associated with them. And there is now abundant evidence that psychiatric disorders themselves are the result of a complex mixture of neurobiological (i.e., brain) dysregulation, psychological stress, and maladaptive coping efforts. One way to think of suicide is that it is the last stage of a psychiatric disorder for some (but not most) people. Another way to say this is: people can literally die of depression or bipolar disorder in the same way they can die of heart disease or cancer.

- *State of Mind.* Another important factor in suicide is the psychological state of mind of the person who is suicidal. We know that a major component of suicidal thinking is a sense of hopelessness. A person who feels unlovable, like they don't belong, helpless, and a burden to others is at higher risk of suicide. In addition, personality traits such as impulsivity or a tendency to react to stress with depressive symptoms, along with a pile-up of stressful events in the person's life (see next item: *Stressors*), such as a being fired from a job or being arrested, appear to create a potentially lethal mix of agitation, desperation, and hopelessness that can lead to a suicide attempt or completion.

- *Stressors.* Stressful events can contribute to the sense of helplessness, hopelessness, and aloneness that can increase the risk for suicide. For example, the loss of relationships such as the break-up of a romance or marriage, or the death of a loved one, can increase risk. Similarly, the loss of what might be called one's "role status" in the community can add to suicidal feelings. For example, becoming unemployed and losing one's role as the breadwinner for a family may increase risk for suicide.

- *Social Factors.* The people around us can also play a role. Such things as social isolation, feeling stigmatized or shunned by others, and physically or emotionally abused by others (such as being bullied) can contribute to the creation of suicidal thoughts and behaviors.

- ***Situational Factors.*** Easy access to a firearm when one is suicidal, or exposure to the suicide of another person, can also play a role in this perfect storm.

As you can see, suicide is a complex phenomenon, and it is never the result of just one thing. It is an unfortunate combination of several factors that all converged at once— in other words, the "perfect storm."

Can Suicide Be Prevented?

Sometimes, well-meaning efforts to prevent suicide make use of slogans such as "Depression is a treatable illness" and "Suicide is preventable." We understand the good intentions behind those efforts. However, it is clear that not all depressions are treatable nor have we yet found a way to prevent all suicides. On the other side of the coin is the belief that "if someone is suicidal and determined to die, there is nothing that anyone can do to stop them." The problem is that these sweeping statements can lead people to believe that psychiatric problems are easily curable, that every suicide attempt can be stopped, or conversely, that we are helpless to even try to stop someone who is suicidal. Unfortunately, they can also contribute to the guilt felt by survivors, who may conclude that "my loved one's death could have been prevented if only I (or someone else) had done the right thing." The truth is that the answers to the problem of suicide prevention are much more complex than these simplistic generalizations would have you believe. What we do know is that some, but not all people can be helped with their depressive feelings and that some, but not all people can be stopped from taking their life. *We need to make every effort to provide effective help to anyone who is suicidal. But society also needs to recognize that not every suicide can be prevented, in spite of our best efforts.*

It follows that if suicide is the perfect storm of the wrong things happening, then perhaps we can say that suicide prevention is the perfect rainbow of the right things happening. The individual who is suicidal must communicate their distress and intentions in some recognizable way - unfortunately, this is often done obliquely, as when an individual begins giving away their possessions, or making statements like "I won't be a burden much longer." Then, the people around the suicidal individual must recognize and react appropriately to the warning signs that someone is contemplating a suicide attempt. After that, the necessary support and professional services must be readily available, not just for the immediate crisis, but to provide longer term follow-up so that the distressed individual receives the competent care that is necessary. Unfortunately, there is considerable evidence that suicidal individuals are often "under-treated" for their psychiatric disorders, social distress, and suicidality – the mental health care system in the United States is frequently deficient in the quantity and quality of services that it provides for suicidal individuals. And lastly, the person who is suicidal has to be able to hold on to the part of themselves that wants to live. We know that most people who take their life are ambivalent about dying, but they have reached a point where they perceive that all of their other options have been exhausted, and that only suicide can solve their problems and resolve their distress. Thus, when all of the elements in the "perfect rainbow" of protective conditions are present, then suicide can indeed be prevented. Tragically, this does not happen often enough. *Suicide prevention efforts in our country must be improved so that help is available when and where people need it, and the public understands and responds appropriately to distress signals from someone who is thinking of ending their life.* For more information suicide prevention efforts in our country, please see the website of the National Action Alliance for Suicide Prevention (http://actionallianceforsuicideprevention.org/).

So, could the suicide of your loved one have been prevented? We know that this question often haunts many survivors for a long time. What we can tell you is that while some suicides can be prevented, *it is rarely within the power of just one person to prevent a suicide* – instead, it takes the collective efforts of mental health professionals, family and friends, and yes, the suicidal person themselves, to keep it from happening. Come back to this fact again and again as you work to understand the suicide of your loved one. Most survivors suffer from what one of our clients – a physician whose son died by suicide – called "the tyranny of hindsight." Looking back on his son's life he could now see some of the warning signs about his son's condition and some of the things that he might have done differently to make a difference. But with time and reflection, he also came to realize that these recognitions were just that: hindsight.

For more information about suicide and about psychiatric disorders, contact:

The National Institute of Mental Health (www.nimh.nih.gov)

The American Foundation for Suicide Prevention (www.afsp.org)

The American Association of Suicidology (www.suicidology.org)

The American Psychiatric Association (www.psych.org)

The American Psychological Association (www.apa.org).

The National Action Alliance for Suicide Prevention (http://actionallianceforsuicideprevention.org/).

APPENDIX C:

Military, Fire, or Emergency Medical Technician (EMT) Suicides

When a person in the military, police, fire or EMT services (or a veteran of those services) ends his or her life, a number of questions arise:

- To what extent did the stress of the military or civilian service contribute to the suicide?
- Were there other contributing factors that go beyond their service experience?
- Were there clues and risk factors that the individual's commanders should have recognized?
- How did the military or civilian services handle the suicide?
- What more can we do to reduce suicides among our service men and women?

One common problem for survivor families who have lost an active duty or retired member to suicide is the issue of stigma. All of these services put a high value on courage, self-sacrifice, and honor. And traditionally, all of them have considered suicide to be a more or less dishonorable way to die. Of course, suicidal behavior, and the family of any person who dies by suicide, is often stigmatized by the rest of society. Unfortunately, this problem is even greater in the military and similar civilian services. Families have traditionally been ostracized by the community that they most need to support them. The good news is that the attitude toward the suicide of military and service personnel is beginning to change, as demonstrated by a growing understanding that:

- Suicide is not a cowardly act, but an act of desperation to control unbearable pain
- The nature of the work often adds additional stressors, although it is rarely the only factor. Suicidal behavior is a sign of someone in need of help from colleagues, not of someone who should be shamed.

- A major factor contributing to suicide in the military and civilian uniformed services is the taboo about seeking help when one has a problem

- An additional issue is the ready access to lethal means, such as firearms

- Finally, there is the tendency for the public to believe the myth that all members of the uniformed services are "super heroes" who do not suffer the same emotional problems or vulnerabilities with which civilians struggle. Of course, this is not true. Members of the military, police, and fire services are human also.

It is one thing for military, police, or fire/rescue personnel to die in the line of duty. But unfortunately, it is viewed quite differently when a person who is sworn to protect others takes their life while on active duty or sometime thereafter. As with all suicides, families are left to ask, "Why?"

If you are in this situation, what can you do? Here are a few suggestions:

- If you haven't already, find ways to be proud of your loved one. Chances are they were fighting an invisible, but no less heroic, battle of their own.

- When you are asked how your loved one died, some family members have found that it is helpful to say something like:

  My loved one died from suicide and was fighting their own inner battle -- unfortunately the battle was lost on [fill in date] _____."

- Look for a place to be able to talk with other family members of service people who have died by suicide. One excellent resource for military families is TAPS (Tragedy Assistance Program for Survivors, www.taps.org/suicide).

- Find a way to work with the services to stem the tide of suicide and make sure that members of the uniformed services get the help they need.

- Continue reading this book for more coping suggestions.

APPENDIX D

For Those Who Wish to Support a Survivor of Suicide Loss

This Appendix is addressed to readers who wish to help a suicide survivor. When we have asked suicide survivors how friends and family helped during the weeks and months after the death, here were some of their answers:

- Learn about the wide variety of ways that survivors cope with a death by suicide.

- Be a good listener—realize that while you can't fix grief, you can listen patiently and compassionately.

- Don't offer empty words of reassurance ("It'll be okay.") or clichés ("I know just how you feel") or false comfort ("She's in heaven now") unless you know *for sure* that these words are going to be of help. The best gift you can give someone who is grieving is to realize that you *do not* know how they feel, but that you are open to having them "teach" you what this experience is like for them. And ask yourself why you are saying what you are saying: is it because the words make *you* feel more comfortable and less awkward, or are they what the other person really needs to hear? When in doubt, you can just say "I don't know what to say to you, except that I am so very, very sorry".

- Tell survivors that you care — and show them.

- Don't be afraid to say the name of the person who died, or tell stories about his or her life.

- Allow the survivor to be in emotional pain. Don't look for a silver lining—there isn't likely to be one, and even if there is, that's for the survivor to discover, not for you to point out to them.

- Don't assume you know what's best for the person. Offer resources (see Appendix F), but let the survivor decide if he or she is ready to use them.

- Allow the survivor to cry and cry — or to shed no tears at all.

- Be ready to hear, over and over, the story of the person who died; the circumstances of the death; and the current problems of the mourner.

- As months go by, don't be afraid to ask, "How are you doing with _____'s death?" If the survivor answers your question, be prepared to simply listen. If the survivor would rather not talk about it at that time, respect that decision too.

- Remember the birthday and death day of the person who died and be sure to send a message, make a call, or mail a card on those days.

- Realize that each person grieves in his or her own way. Allow the person to feel whatever emotions arise. This includes guilt, anger, and sadness.

- Find practical ways to help the survivor, such as offering to do errands, watching the kids, mowing the lawn, driving the survivor to an appointment, helping with chores, accompanying them to church, or simply sitting quietly with the survivor.

- Ask the survivor directly, "How can I help you? What do you need?"

- Watch for unhealthy grief reactions and suggest counseling, if needed. Otherwise, accept what may seem to you to be a prolonged period of intense grief reactions.

- Don't set a timetable for the survivor to be "over it" or "back to normal." If the survivor seems to have an upsurge of grief even many years later, let the person know that this is usually quite normal. Realize that the suicide has changed this person forever, and that the survivor may carry aspects of grief for the rest of his or her life. Suicide survivors will never be the people they used to be, but they can become stronger and more compassionate as a result of their tragedy.

APPENDIX E

If You Are Concerned About Someone Being Suicidal (Including Yourself)

In addition to the sorrow and trauma that it leaves behind, one of the most distressing things about suicide is that it can sometimes leave survivors feeling suicidal themselves. Exposure to both suicidal behavior and to the suicide completion of a loved one is associated with a somewhat elevated risk for the same behavior in the survivor. This can happen to people at any age. As we mentioned in the main text, our advice to survivors about this issue is: *you should be more vigilant about suicide in someone who is a survivor, but not terrified. Having said that, losing someone to suicide does not, in any way, mean that you or someone else who was exposed to the suicide is "doomed" to die by suicide.*

So, how can you know if you or someone you care about is at risk for suicide, and what can you do if you feel that they are in need of help? In Appendix E, we will cover four topics: *the overall risk of suicide in survivors, risk factors for suicide, warning signs of imminent danger of a suicide attempt, and steps to take if you believe that someone is suicidal. Risk of suicide in survivors* refers to the question "In general, are suicide survivors at greater risk for suicide themselves? If so, how much greater?" *Risk factors* are past and present events that are associated with elevated suicide risk over a long period of time. For example, people with a history of traumatic abuse in their childhood have a somewhat greater risk of becoming suicidal at some point in their life. Likewise, individuals suffering from depression or bipolar disorder have a greater chance of becoming suicidal (although it is important to know that most people who experience these psychiatric disorders do not become suicidal). *Warning signs* are markers that someone may be acutely at risk, and that it may well be time to take action to help them be safe and get the professional attention they need. We will describe these risk factors and warning signs for someone else, but you can apply them equally well to yourself if you are concerned about your own mental health. *Steps to take* will include simple and straight-forward actions that you can take to get help for yourself or someone you care about.

Risk of suicide in Survivors

The question of risk for suicide is an important one for all of our society, but it has a special meaning for those who have lost a loved one to suicide. Survivors often worry "Am I now at risk for suicide?" or "My children's father took his life – are they now going to do the same thing?" We addressed this in the main text by encouraging you to be more vigilant about the presence of a psychiatric disorder in your loved ones (particularly mood disorders such as depression and bipolar disorder). Here we would like to give you a summary of the epidemiological data on the risk of suicide in people who have been exposed to the suicide of someone close to them.

Elevated risk for suicide depends on a number of factors, including the relationship between the deceased and the survivor. On a statistical basis and across all survivor categories (i.e., bereaved parents, children, siblings, spouses, etc.), the overall risk for suicide is between two and three times greater for survivors than for the population at large. Before you panic, however, it is important to remember that despite what has happened to you, completed suicide is a relatively rare phenomenon. As we noted in Appendix B, the data about suicide in the U.S. indicates that about 12 people out of every 100,000 will die by suicide in a given year. Contrast this with the fact that the death rate for cancer in the U.S. is about 180 per 100,000 – about 15 times the rate of death from suicide. So, to say that survivors are two or three times more likely to die by suicide than the general population means that the suicide rate for survivors is about 30/100,000 – still a pretty low number.

We do know that some groups of suicide survivors are generally at higher risk for completing suicide than others. For example, elderly men who have lost their wives to suicide are at significantly higher risk for suicide themselves. Also, survivors who prior to the death of their loved one also had a history of being suicidal themselves are at higher risk. This is particularly true if the survivor has made previous suicide attempts. Why are survivors at higher risk for suicide than the population at large? One likely reason for this is that, at least for biologically related family members, they share a similar genetic make-up. It is well established that many psychiatric disorders have some amount of "genetic loading," meaning that the disorder is to some extent caused by the genetic make-up of the individual – most likely by creating a kind of neurobiological vulnerability to trauma and stressful events. But even for people who have no shared genetics (for example, husbands and wives, or adolescents who are exposed to the suicide of a peer), simply being exposed to suicidal behavior seems to somewhat elevate the risk. This is probably a result of a kind of "role-modeling effect," in which suicide as a means of dealing with psychological stress becomes more acceptable when we see someone else using this method to deal with their own pain.

So let us reiterate what we said in the main text: if you have lost someone close to you to suicide, then you or someone else close to the deceased is at somewhat greater risk of becoming suicidal themselves. But the risk is not dramatically higher. We encourage you, then, to be vigilant about a psychiatric disorder in your loved ones. We also encourage you to educate yourself about the risk factors and warning signs of suicide, and to be proactive about seeking help for yourself or someone else about whom you are concerned. The information that follows next will help you assess this risk.

Risk Factors for Suicide

Here are some of the factors that, over an individual's lifetime, may increase their risk for suicidal thoughts or behaviors.

- Family history of suicidal behavior or completion in an immediate family member
- History of previous suicidal behavior or harm to oneself
- History of psychiatric disorders (particularly mood disorders such as depression or bipolar disorder). Other disorders with increased risk of suicide include Post Traumatic Stress Disorder, psychotic disorders (such as schizophrenia), borderline personality disorder, panic disorder, conduct, or anti-social personality disorders, and eating disorders.

- History of trauma and/or abuse, particularly chronic abuse by a caregiver in childhood or adolescence, including sexual abuse.
- History of violent, reckless, or impulsive behaviors
- Certain medical conditions such as epilepsy, traumatic brain injury, recent diagnosis of a life-threatening illness, and diseases or injuries that create chronic pain.
- Substance abuse disorder involving alcohol, street drugs, and abuse of prescription drugs
- Chronic low self-esteem or self-loathing
- Recent losses such as divorce, death of a spouse, or job loss.

It is important to note that by themselves, no single one of these risk factors indicates that the person will make a suicide attempt during their lifetime. ***Many people who have one or more of these risk factors never make an attempt, or even consider suicide.*** However, it is also true that the greater the number of these risk factors that are present, the greater the chances that an individual may become suicidal.

Warning Signs of Imminent Risk

Here are some signs that an individual may be at acute risk for making a suicide attempt:

- Preoccupation with suicide or a wish to be dead
- Verbal threats of self-harm or suicide – talk of suicide, including a plan or method for suicide
- Seeking or acquiring the means for suicide (example – purchasing a firearm)
- A recent suicide attempt
- Increased use of alcohol or other drugs
- Significant and worsening depressed mood – particularly when accompanied by hopelessness
- Aggressive, reckless, risk-taking, or revenge-seeking behavior
- Recent discharge from a psychiatric hospitalization, particularly for suicidal behavior

- Severe anhedonia - the inability to feel pleasure
- Agitation as shown by restless anxiety, persistent nightmares, or increasing irritability
- Intolerable emotional states resulting from panic attacks, feelings of deep despair and hopelessness, shame and public humiliation, or unremitting guilt
- Physiological dysregulation such as sleeping too much or too little
- Dramatic changes in mood. This includes a sudden improvement in mood for someone who has been depressed. The apparent improvement may be because the person has made a plan to end their pain through suicide.
- Withdrawal from other people and activities, "leave-taking" behaviors such as saying good-bye, giving things away, taking out life insurance and making a will
- Psychotic symptoms as demonstrated by hallucinations (such as hearing voices demanding suicide) or paranoia
- Perceived sense of being a burden on other people or of not belonging
- Being threatened at home, school, or work
- Being a victim of domestic violence and/or rape

It is important to repeat that, by themselves, no single one of these warning signs indicates that the person is about to make a suicide attempt. Instead, a combination of these signs and an increasing severity of the signs indicate that a crisis is developing and protective action may be needed.

Steps to Take If You Believe That Someone Is at Risk

Here are some steps to take if you believe that someone is at risk for making a suicide attempt:

- ASK! – *Please* do not be afraid to ask someone if they are wishing that they were dead or thinking of suicide. You will not put the idea into their head, and most likely they will be relieved that you noticed their distress and cared enough to inquire. *Take all threats of suicide seriously.*

Important questions to ask include:

1. Do you wish that you were dead?
2. Are you thinking of killing yourself?
3. Have you made the decision that you are going to end your life?
4. Do you have a plan?
5. Can you see alternatives to taking your life?
6. Do you have a time and place in which you intend to attempt?
7. Do you have the means to make a suicide attempt?
8. If you have the means, where is it now?
9. What is the one thing that might help you change your mind?

- LISTEN! – encourage the individual to talk about the thoughts and feelings they are having, and what they are planning. Listen carefully, without judging the person's way of looking at their situation. *Do not* try to argue with the individual about whether suicide is "justified" or whether they have reasons to live. Instead, express your concern for the amount of distress they are feeling and your wish to help them get help. A statement such as, "You have been dealing with a lot in your life and I know that it may seem hopeless right now, but let's get you some help" can go a long way towards showing the person how much you care and steer them toward getting the help they need.

- EXPRESS! – your empathy for the distress they are feeling, concern for their well-being, and willingness to try to help.

- ENCOURAGE! – encourage them to get help quickly. Offer to call a family member or good friend. Ask if they are in treatment and offer to contact their clinician. If not in treatment, offer to help them find help. ***Contact the 24-hour Suicide Help line at 1-800-273-TALK (8255) from anywhere in the United***

States to receive confidential help and referral for yourself or someone else.

- REMOVE! – With the person's cooperation, remove any means to make an attempt in the person's environment, particularly firearms.

- STAY! –Stay with the person until both of you have put together a plan to keep them safe, which includes getting help from a professional. To repeat: do not leave the individual alone until resources are in place to keep the person safe. If necessary, take the individual to the emergency department of the nearest hospital, or call 911 for immediate help.

- FOLLOW – UP! – If possible, check back with the individual to see how they are doing. Show your concern and willingness to help.

REMEMBER: When In Doubt, Call 1-800-273-TALK (8255)

For additional information about helping someone who is suicidal, see:

- The National Suicide Prevention Lifeline: 1-800-273-TALK (8255) or www.suicidepreventionlifeline.org

- American Foundation for Suicide Prevention: www.afsp.org/SOP

- American Association of Suicidology: www.suicidology.org

APPENDIX F
SURVIVING AFTER SUICIDE LOSS
Recommended Readings & Resources for Survivors

_Bolton, Iris *My Son...My Son: A Guide to Healing After Death, Loss or Suicide* Atlanta, GA: Bolton Press, 1983.

_Cammarata, Doreen *Someone I Love Died by Suicide: A Story for Child Survivors and Those Who Care for Them.* Grief Guidance, Inc., 2001. (www.griefguidance.com).

Collins, Judy *Sanity and Grace: A Journey of Suicide, Survival, and Strength.* Tarcher/Penguin, 2003.

Colt, George Howe *November of the Soul: The Enigma of Suicide* New York: Scribner: Books, 2006.

_Dougy Center for Grieving Children. *After Suicide: A Workbook for Grieving Kids.* Dougy Center, 2001 (www.dougy.org/).

_Feigelman, W., Jordan, J.R., McIntosh, J, & Feigelman, B. (2012) *Devastating Losses: How Parents Cope With the Death of a Child to Suicide or Drugs.* New York, NY: Springer Publishers.

_Fine, Carla *No Time to Say Good-Bye: Surviving the Suicide of a Loved One* New York: Doubleday, 1997.

_Goldman, Linda *Great Answers to Difficult Questions about Death: What Children Need to Know about Death* Jessica Philadelphia, PA: Jessica Kingsley Publishers, 2009.

_Jamison, Kay Redfield *An Unquiet Mind: A Memoir of Moods and Madness.* New York, NY: Knopf, 1995

_Jamison, Kay Redfield *Night Falls Fast: Understanding Suicide.* New York, NY: Knopf, 1999.

_Joiner, Thomas *Myths About Suicide* Cambridge, MA: Harvard University Press, 2011.

_Joiner, Thomas *Why People Die by Suicide* Cambridge, MA: Harvard University Press, 2006.

_Kosminsky, Phyllis *Getting Back to Life When Grief Won't Heal* New York, NY: McGraw-Hill, 2007.

_Lester, David *Making Sense of Suicide: An In-Depth Look at Why People Kill Themselves* Philadelphia, PA: Charles Press, 1997.

_Linn-Gust, M., & Cerel, J. *Seeking Hope: Stories of the Suicide Bereaved* (Eds.). Albuquerque: Chellehead Works (2011).

_Linn-Gust, M., & Peters, J. (2010). *A Winding Road: A Handbook for Those Supporting the Suicide Bereaved.* Albuquerque: Chellehead Works, 2010.

_Linn-Gust, M. *Rocky Roads: The Journeys of Families through Suicide Grief.* Albuquerque, NM: Chellehead Works, 2010.

_Linn-Gust, M. *Do they have bad days in heaven? Surviving the suicide loss of a sibling.* Atlanta, GA: Bolton Press, 2001 (Chellehead Works 2002).

_Marcus, Eric *Why Suicide?* New York, NY: Harper-Collins, 2010.

_Meyers, Michael & Fine, Carla *Touched by Suicide: Hope and Healing After Loss* New York, NY: Gotham Books, 2006.

_Rappaport, Nancy *In Her Wake: A Child Psychiatrist Explores the Mystery of Her Mother's Suicide* New York, NY: Basic Books, 2009.

_Requarth, Margo *After a Parent's Suicide: Helping Children Heal.* Sebastopol, CA: Healing Hearts Press, 2006 (www.HealingHeartsPress.com).

_Rubel, Barbara. *But I Didn't Say Goodbye: For Parents and Professionals Helping Child Suicide Survivors.* Griefwork Center, Inc. 2000.

_Slaby, Andrew & Garfinkel, Lili *No One Saw My Pain: Why Teens Kill Themselves* New York, NY: W.W. Norton & Co., 1994.

_ Solomon, Andrew *The Noonday Demon: An Atlas of Depression* New York, NY: Scribner, 2001.

_Styron, William *Darkness Visible: A Memoir of Madness.* New York, NY: Random House, 1990.

_Wise, Terry L. *Waking Up-Climbing Through The Darkness* Oxnard, CA: Pathfinder Publishing, 2004.

_Wrobleski, A. & Reidenberg, D. *Suicide: Why? 85 Questions and Answers*, 3rd Ed. SAVE (Suicide Awareness Voices of Education), 2005. (http://www.save.org/)

Book Services:
These book services specialize in a wide range of books related to loss and bereavement, for children, adolescents, and adults.

_ Compassion Books Burnsville, NC – Telephone - 1-800-970-4220 http://www.compassionbooks.com/store/

_ Centering Corporation – Omaha, NE – Telephone - 866-218-0101 http://www.centering.org/

Organizations and Online Resources:
All of these groups have resources for survivors.

_Alliance of Hope - http://www.allianceofhope.org/alliance-of-hope-for-suic/welcome.html - an excellent online resource for survivors that is moderated by trained peer survivors.

_American Association of Suicidology - 5221 Wisconsin Avenue, NW Washington, DC 20015 Telephone 202-237-2280. www.suicidology.org/

_American Foundation for Suicide Prevention 120 Wall Street – 29th Floor, New York, NY-10005 Telephone 888-363-3500. www.afsp.org/

_Center for Suicide Prevention Suite 320, 1202 Centre Street S.E. Calgary, AB T2G 5A5, Canada – Telephone: 403-245-3900. http://suicideinfo.ca/.

_National Action Alliance for Suicide Prevention – a public-private partnership formed in 2010 to advance the U.S. National Strategy for Suicide Prevention – within the NAASP, the Survivors of Suicide Loss Task Force has issued National Guidelines for helping people after a suicide. – see this link: http://actionallianceforsuicideprevention.org/sites/actionallianceforsuicideprevention.org/files/NationalGuidelines.pdf - Appendix E of this document contains an excellent list of all types of resources for survivors.

_ Parents of Suicide and Friends and Families of Suicide - http://www.pos-ffos.com/ - online web resources for parents bereaved by suicide, and other family members/friends bereaved by suicide (siblings, children, spouses, friends, etc.).

_ SAVE (Suicide Awareness Voices of Education) - 8120 Penn Ave. S., Suite 470, Bloomington, MN – 55431 – Telephone 952- 946-7998.

_Sibling Survivors.com - http://siblingsurvivors.com/sibling-grief/ - for survivors of the death of a sibling to suicide.

_ Suicide: Finding Hope - http://www.suicidefindinghope.com/

_ Suicide Grief Support: Quick Reference – a comprehensive listing of support resources for suicide survivors. - https://sites.google.com/a/personalgriefcoach.com/suicidegriefsupport/ or sg.sg/griefreference

_Suicide Grief Support Forum - http:www.suicidegrief.com

Acknowledgments

We thank the following people for their valuable input in reading drafts of this book. Thanks also to the people who contributed their stories and endorsements. We are sincerely grateful for the time all these folks took to help make this a book a valuable resource for people coping with the grief of a suicide.

Jean Abel	Vanessa McGann
Paige Alvord	Jack McMahon
Peggy Anderson	Mary Pat McMahon
Janet Bardle	AnneMarie Mahoney
Iris Bolton	Gerard Mahoney
David Breakstone	Eric Marcus
Ron Callahan	Peggy Marshall
Franklin Cook	Kathryn Melsness
Lew Cox	Christine Moutier
Rob Desmond	Monica Nunes
Debbie DiMasi	Anita Pandolfe-Ruchman
Carole Duncan	Jim Peta
Heather Dwyer	Pat Peta
Sue Eastgard	Nancy Rappaport
Laura Edwards	Kim Ruocco
Nancy Ekdahl	Colleen Ryan
Linda Fehrmann	Trudy Sevier
Bill & Beverly Feigelman	Kristen Spexarth
Ruth Hargiss	Suzanne Stevens
Joanne Harpel	Dennis Tackett
Jane Jackson	Kristen Young
Shirley Kaminsky	Mary Young
Kristine Kuch	

We also would like to thank Ms. Madeline Drexler, who provided editorial assistance with the final draft of the first edition of this book. Thanks also to our printer, Ron Engstrom, and to Bob's wife, Kris, for their computer and production expertise and artwork on the cover in preparing this book for printing.

About the Authors

Jack Jordan is a psychologist in private practice in Pawtucket, RI. He is the Clinical Consultant for Grief Support Services of the Samaritans in Boston, MA, and the Professional Advisor to the Loss and Bereavement Council of the American Foundation for Suicide Prevention. For over 30 years, Jack has provided training nationally and internationally for professional caregivers, and has helped to lead many healing workshops for suicide loss survivors. Jack has published over 50 clinical and research articles and chapters, and he is the co-author of three other books: "Grief After Suicide: Coping with the Consequences and Caring for the Survivors", "Devastating Losses: How Parents Cope With the Death of a Child to Suicide or Drugs"; and "Attachment Informed Grief Therapy".

Bob Baugher is an instructor at Highline College in Des Moines, Washington where he teaches courses in Psychology and Death Education. Through the Livingworks organization he has trained more than 1,000 people in suicide intervention. As a bereavement counselor and group facilitator, Bob has helped people who have experienced the death of a child, sibling, parent, partner, and friend. He has earned a Fellow in Thanatology through the Association for Death Education and Counseling and has given more than 800 workshops in coping with grief. The author of seven other books, Bob has served as the professional advisor for the South King County chapter of the Compassionate Friends (a bereaved parent organization). Bob's website is www.bobbaugher@wordpress.com.

Discounts for Ordering Multiple Copies

2-10 copies:	5% Discount
11-24 copies:	10% Discount
25-49 copies:	20% Discount
50-99 copies:	30% Discount
100 copies or more:	35% Discount

Price: $15.00 (U.S. funds) per copy.
Free shipping in the U.S.
Out of U.S. rate: Shipping billed according to postal rates.

Washington state residents add 10.1% sales tax.

Please allow 1-2 weeks for delivery.

Send Check or Money Order payable to:

Bob or Kris Baugher
7108 127th Place SE
Newcastle, WA 98056   OR

e-mail your order and you will be billed:

b_kbaugher@yahoo.com

Visit our website at www.bobbaugher.com

Other books by Dr. Baugher:

- Coping with Grief: *A Guide for the Bereaved Survivor* – $10.00

- Coping with Grief (Spanish version) – $10.00

- *Understanding Guilt During Bereavement* – $10.00

- *Death Turns Allie's Family Upside Down*
  with Linda Wong-Garl & Kris Baugher – $10.00

- *Understanding Anger During Bereavement*
  with Carol Hankins, M.S. and Gary Hankins, Ph.D. – $8.00

- *Coping with Traumatic Death: Homicide* with Lew Cox – $10.00

- *Coping with Traumatic Death: Homicide* (Spanish version) – $10.00

- *The Crying Handbook* with Darcie Sims, Ph.D. – $10.00

- *In the Midst of Caregiving* with Darcie Sims, Ph.D. – $12.00

- *Men and their Grief DVD* – $25.00

- *Men and their Grief–20 Years Later DVD* – $25.00

- *Men and their Grief–Double Set* – $40.00